Making Sense of the Stock Market

One Term at a Time

A Clear and Practical Guide to Stock Market Terms, Definitions, and Concepts Explained in Simple, Everyday Language

Published by: **SB Books**

Printed in the United States of America.

ISBN: 979-8-9928807-8-6

Trademarks:

All business terms, stock market terms, company names, logos, and trademarks referenced in this book are the property of their respective owners. Use of these names is for identification and educational purposes only and does not imply endorsement..

Disclaimer:

This book is provided for educational purposes only. It is not intended to provide business, legal, tax, accounting, financial, or professional advice related to investing or the stock market. Market conditions, regulations, and financial practices may change over time. Readers should verify current information and consult qualified financial professionals before making any investment or financial decisions. Neither SB Books nor Prosperity Pathways LLC assumes responsibility for actions taken based on the information contained in this book

Limitation of Liability:

The information in this book is provided without any guarantees or warranties, express or implied. The author and publisher shall not be held responsible for any losses, damages, or consequences resulting from the use of the material presented herein, including but not limited to financial or investment losses.

The stock market shapes wealth, opportunity, and financial decisions.

But its basics are rarely taught in a simple way.

Table of Contents

1. What Is the Stock Market? 1
2. What Is the Purpose of the Stock Market? 2
3. What Are Capital Markets? 3
4. What Are Equity Markets? 4
5. What Are Public Companies? 5
6. What Is Ownership Through Stocks? 6
7. What Are Shareholders? 7
8. What Are Investors? 8
9. What Are Issuers? 9
10. What Are Market Participants? 10
11. What Is a Stock Exchange? 11
12. What Is the New York Stock Exchange? 12
13. What Is NASDAQ? 13
14. What Is the Primary Market? 14
15. What Is the Secondary Market? 15
16. What Is Listing? 16
17. What Are Listing Requirements? 17
18. What Is an Initial Public Offering (IPO)? 18
19. What Is a Direct Listing? 19
20. What Is Delisting? 20
21. What Is a Brokerage Account? 21
22. What Is a Broker? 22
23. What Is an Online Brokerage? 23
24. What Is a Full-Service Broker? 24
25. What Is a Discount Broker? 25
26. What Is Market Access? 26
27. What Are Clearing and Settlement? 27
28. What Is the Settlement Period? 28
29. What Is Custody of Securities? 29
30. What Are Account Types? 30
31. What Is a Buy Order? 31
32. What Is a Sell Order? 32
33. What Is a Market Order? 33
34. What Is a Limit Order? 34
35. What Is a Stop Order? 35
36. What Is a Stop-Loss Order? 36

37. What Is Order Execution? 37
38. What Is Order Routing? 38
39. What Are Bid and Ask? 39
40. What Is the Bid-Ask Spread? 40
41. What Is Market Price? 41
42. What Is Price Discovery? 42
43. What Is Supply and Demand? 43
44. What Is Liquidity? 44
45. What Is Trading Volume? 45
46. What Is Volatility? 46
47. What Is Price Efficiency? 47
48. What Is Market Depth? 48
49. What Are Thinly Traded Stocks? 49
50. What Is Price Impact? 50
51. What Is Market Capitalization? 51
52. What Are Large-Cap Stocks? 52
53. What Are Mid-Cap Stocks? 53
54. What Are Small-Cap Stocks? 54
55. What Are Micro-Cap Stocks? 55
56. What Are Outstanding Shares? 56
57. What Is Public Float? 57
58. What Is Free Float? 58
59. What Are Share Classes? 59
60. What Are Dual-Class Shares? 60
61. What Is Investment Return? 61
62. What Are Capital Gains? 62
63. What Are Dividends? 63
64. What Is Dividend Yield? 64
65. What Is Dividend Policy? 65
66. What Is Total Return? 66
67. What Is Reinvestment? 67
68. What Is a Holding Period? 68
69. What Is Compounding? 69
70. What Are Long-Term Returns? 70
71. What Is a Bull Market? 71
72. What Is a Bear Market? 72
73. What Is a Market Cycle? 73
74. What Is a Market Correction? 74
75. What Is a Market Crash? 75

76. What Is Market Recovery? 76
77. What Are Economic Cycles? 77
78. What Is Interest Rate Impact? 78
79. What Is Inflation Impact? 79
80. What Is Global Market Influence? 80
81. What Are Earnings? 81
82. What Are Earnings Reports? 82
83. What Is Revenue? 83
84. What Is Profit? 84
85. What Are Financial Statements? 85
86. What Is Valuation? 86
87. What Is the Price-to-Earnings (P/E) Ratio? 87
88. What Are Growth Stocks? 88
89. What Are Value Stocks? 89
90. What Are Market Expectations? 90
91. What Is Market Risk? 91
92. What Is Company-Specific Risk? 92
93. What Is Systemic Risk? 93
94. What Is Diversification? 94
95. What Is Regulation? 95
96. What Is Market Oversight? 96
97. What Is Investor Protection? 97
98. What Is Behavioral Bias? 98
99. What Is Market Efficiency? 99
100. What Is Stock Market Reality? 100

INTRODUCTION

The stock market is a major part of modern life, yet many people go through school and adulthood without ever being clearly taught how it works. Terms like stocks, shares, market price, volatility, dividends, and investing are used constantly, but often without simple explanations. As a result, the stock market can feel confusing, unpredictable, or even intimidating—especially for those trying to understand how it actually operates.

Making Sense of the Stock Market was created to bring clarity to these core concepts. This book explains essential stock market terms in clear, straightforward language. The goal is not to turn readers into traders or analysts, but to help them understand how the stock market works in real life.

You will learn what common stock market terms truly mean, where they appear in real situations, and why they matter. The focus is on practical understanding—how investing works, how prices move, how people participate in the market. Each concept is explained step by step, using relatable examples that make abstract ideas easier to understand.

For readers who want to continue learning beyond this book, additional resources and simple guides are available at www.buildwealthretirerich.com.

This book builds a strong foundation by breaking down key ideas into simple explanations. When you understand the fundamentals, more advanced investing topics become easier to navigate.

Whether you are a student, beginner investor, professional, or simply someone who wants to understand the stock market with confidence, this book provides a practical foundation.

1. What Is the Stock Market?

Overview

The stock market is a system where shares of public companies are bought and sold. A share is a small piece of ownership in a company. When you buy a share, you become a part-owner, even if it is a tiny slice. The stock market is not a store where companies "sell products." It is a marketplace where investors trade ownership pieces of companies with each other.

You'll hear about the stock market in news headlines, investing apps, and retirement accounts. Understanding it helps you make sense of market movements and your investments.

Example

Imagine a company called Bright Bottle becomes a public company and has 1,000 shares available for investors to own. You buy 10 shares. That means you own 10/1,000 of the company. Later, another investor wants to buy those shares from you and offers a higher price than what you paid. If you sell to that investor, you make a profit. If the price is lower, you would take a loss. This buying and selling between investors is what happens in the stock market every day.

Why This Matters

- The stock market is where ownership in public companies is traded, so it affects many investments and retirement accounts.
- People often confuse "the stock market" with "the economy," but they are not the same thing.
- Understanding the stock market helps you interpret market news, price changes, and what it means to be a shareholder.

Key Takeaway

The stock market is a marketplace where people buy and sell small ownership pieces of public companies.

2. What Is the Purpose of the Stock Market?

Overview

The stock market connects companies that need money with people who want to invest. Companies sell shares to raise funds for growth, while investors buy them hoping the company becomes more valuable over time.

You'll see this in terms like IPOs, companies "going public," or "raising capital." Many retirement plans and investing apps rely on this process.

It's not just gambling or random numbers—it's a system that helps businesses grow and lets investors share in that growth.

Example

A fast-growing company wants to open new locations but does not want to borrow a huge loan. It sells shares to the public to raise money. Investors buy those shares because they believe the company will grow. The company gets funding, and investors get a chance to benefit if the company succeeds.

Why This Matters

- The stock market affects how many companies raise money and expand
- People often confuse stock price movement with "no real purpose," which can cause fear or bad decisions
- Understanding the purpose helps you see why investing can build long-term wealth

Key Takeaway

The stock market helps companies raise money and gives investors a way to share in a company's growth.

3. What Are Capital Markets?

Overview

Capital markets are the broader system where businesses and governments raise long-term money. "Capital" here means money used to fund big goals like building factories, expanding services, or running large projects. Capital markets include both the stock market and the bond market.

You may hear "capital markets" in business news, in discussions about "raising capital," or when people talk about stocks and bonds together. It is a big umbrella term that describes where long-term investing and long-term fundraising happen.

If you do not understand capital markets, it can be confusing why some investments are called "equity" and others are called "debt," or why companies sometimes sell shares and other times borrow through bonds.

Example

A city wants to build a new bridge. It raises long-term money by issuing bonds. Meanwhile, a company wants to expand nationwide, so it raises money by selling stock. Both are using capital markets to fund long-term plans.

Why This Matters

- It explains how big projects and business growth are financed over time
- Confusing stocks and bonds can lead to mismatched expectations about risk and returns
- Understanding the umbrella helps you organize investing terms more clearly

Key Takeaway

Capital markets are where long-term money is raised through stocks and bonds.

4. What Are Equity Markets?

Overview

Equity markets are the part of capital markets where ownership is bought and sold. "Equity" means ownership. When you buy a company's stock, you are buying equity in that company.

You see equity markets when you look up stock prices, buy shares through a brokerage account, or hear someone say "the equity market was up today." When people talk about "investing in equities," they usually mean investing in stocks.

If you do not understand equity markets, you might think stocks are just "prices on a screen." The key point is that stocks represent ownership, and the price is what people currently agree that ownership is worth.

Example

Two investors trade shares of a public company during the day. One is selling because they want cash for another goal. The other is buying because they believe the company will grow. That trading is happening in the equity market.

Why This Matters

- Many long-term investing strategies rely heavily on equities
- Confusing equity with "a guaranteed profit" can lead to disappointment when prices drop
- Knowing equity means ownership helps you understand what you actually hold

Key Takeaway

Equity markets are where ownership in companies (stocks) is bought and sold.

5. What Are Public Companies?

Overview

Public companies are companies that sell shares to the public and have those shares traded on stock exchanges. This usually happens after the company decides to "go public," meaning regular investors can buy and sell ownership shares.

You encounter public companies every time you see a stock ticker, a company listed on an exchange, or headlines about earnings reports. Public companies also share more financial information with the public than private companies because investors need details to make decisions.

If you misunderstand what "public company" means, you might assume it is owned by the government or open to anyone to visit. Here, "public" simply means the company's shares are available for the public to buy and sell.

Example

A well-known company sells shares on an exchange. You can open a brokerage account, buy one share, and become a small owner. The company must regularly report results so investors can judge how it is performing.

Why This Matters

- Public companies are the main companies you invest in through the stock market
- People often confuse "public" with "government-owned," which is incorrect
- Understanding public companies helps you understand stock listings, reports, and market news

Key Takeaway

A public company is a company whose shares can be bought and sold by the public on the stock market.

6. What Is Ownership Through Stocks?

Overview

Ownership through stocks means that when you buy a company's stock, you own a small piece of that company. That ownership is real, even if it is tiny. It is not the same as "loaning money" to the company. When you own stock, you are an owner, not a lender.

People see this idea in brokerage apps, in retirement accounts, and in news stories that say someone "owns shares" of a company. It also shows up when a company's stock price changes, because the market is constantly updating what that ownership is worth.

If you misunderstand stock ownership, you might expect guaranteed returns or think you can't lose money. Ownership can grow in value, shrink in value, and sometimes pay dividends, depending on how the company performs and how investors feel about its future.

Example

You buy 5 shares of a company at $20 each. You now own a small part of that company. If the stock price rises to $25, your ownership is worth more. If the price drops to $15, your ownership is worth less.

Why This Matters

- Stocks represent ownership, not a promise of profit
- Confusing ownership with "guaranteed money" can lead to bad decisions
- Knowing what you own helps you stay calmer when prices move

Key Takeaway

Buying stock means buying a small piece of ownership in a company.

7. What Are Shareholders?

Overview

Shareholders are the people or groups that own shares of a company. If you own even one share, you are a shareholder. Shareholders can be individuals, retirement accounts, mutual funds, pension funds, or large investing firms.

From a technical perspective, shareholders have a residual claim on the company's assets and earnings. They may also have rights such as voting on key decisions (like electing the board of directors) and receiving dividends if the company distributes profits. Ownership can be direct (through your brokerage account) or indirect (through funds like index funds or ETFs).

You commonly hear "shareholders" in company news, earnings updates, and phrases like "shareholder meeting" or "shareholder value." In everyday life, you may be a shareholder without realizing it if your retirement plan owns stock funds.

Example

A teacher invests in a retirement plan that holds a stock index fund. That fund owns shares of many companies. The teacher is indirectly a shareholder in those companies through the fund.

Why This Matters

- Shareholders are the owners of a company
- Many people are shareholders through retirement accounts
- Understanding this helps you connect investing to real ownership

Key Takeaway

A shareholder is anyone who owns shares of a company, either directly or through a fund.

8. What Are Investors?

Overview

Investors are people or groups who put money into something today because they expect it may be worth more in the future, or may pay income over time. In the stock market, investors buy stocks because they believe the company can grow, become more valuable, or pay dividends.

You see the word "investor" everywhere: in apps, in market news, and in conversations like "investors were nervous today" or "investors liked the earnings report." Investors can be long-term (holding for years) or short-term (buying and selling sooner).

If you confuse investors with traders, you might assume all investing is fast and risky. Many investors focus on long-term growth and use the stock market as a slow-building tool, not a quick win.

Example

Two people buy the same stock. One plans to hold it for 10 years because they believe the company will grow. The other plans to sell next week if the price jumps. Both are investors, but their time horizons are different.

Why This Matters

- "Investor behavior" affects stock prices and market headlines
- Mixing up investing and quick trading can cause unrealistic expectations
- A long-term investor mindset supports better decisions

Key Takeaway

An investor puts money in today to try to build value over time.

9. What Are Issuers?

Overview

Issuers are organizations that create and sell financial securities to raise money. In the stock market, an issuer is usually a company that issues stock shares. Governments and corporations can also issue bonds, but in a stock market basics book, you will most often see issuers as companies offering shares.

You may hear "issuer" in investing account documents, stock offering news, or descriptions of an IPO. The word is used to identify who created the security and who received money when it was first sold.

If you misunderstand "issuer," you might think it refers to the stock exchange or the brokerage app. The issuer is the company (or organization) that originally put the shares into the world.

Example

A company decides to go public and sells shares for the first time. In that moment, the company is the issuer of those shares. Later, when investors trade shares with each other, the issuer is not receiving money from those trades.

Why This Matters

- Issuers raise money by selling shares in the first place
- Many people think companies earn money every time a stock is traded (usually they do not)
- Knowing the issuer helps you understand how stock offerings work

Key Takeaway

An issuer is the company or organization that creates and sells the shares.

10. What Are Market Participants?

Overview

Market participants are all the people and organizations involved in the stock market. This includes individual investors, big institutions (like mutual funds and pension funds), brokers, stock exchanges, and companies that issue shares. Each participant plays a different role, but together they create buying and selling activity that sets stock prices.

You encounter market participants anytime you place a trade in an app (you are a participant), read about "institutional investors," or hear that "the market reacted" to news. That "reaction" is really participants buying and selling based on what they believe.

If you think "the market" is a single thing, it can feel mysterious. It is actually just a crowd of participants making decisions at the same time.

Example

A company reports strong earnings. Some participants buy because they expect growth. Others sell because they think the stock is already expensive. The stock price moves based on the combined actions of all these participants.

Why This Matters

- Prices move because participants react to information and expectations
- Understanding "who is in the market" makes headlines less confusing
- It helps you see that markets are driven by decisions, not magic

Key Takeaway

Market participants are everyone who takes part in buying, selling, and running the stock market.

11. What Is a Stock Exchange?

Overview

A stock exchange is an organized marketplace where stocks are bought and sold. It provides a place (and a set of rules) that helps buyers and sellers trade shares in a clear, orderly way. A stock exchange is not the same as a company, and it is not the same as a brokerage app. Your app is a tool you use to place trades. The exchange is one of the places where those trades can be matched and completed.

People often encounter this term when they see "listed on an exchange," when they look up a stock quote, or when they hear that a company trades on the NYSE or NASDAQ. The exchange matters because it helps create trust: prices are visible, trading follows rules, and information is shared widely.

If you ignore what an exchange is, it can be confusing why companies must meet listing requirements, why trading happens during market hours, and why the same company is "listed" in a specific place.

Example

A company's shares are listed on a stock exchange. Many investors place buy and sell orders through their brokerage apps. The exchange matches buyers and sellers, and the stock price moves as trades happen.

Why This Matters

- Exchanges help make trading fair and organized
- People often confuse a brokerage app with the exchange itself
- Knowing the exchange helps you understand where stocks trade and why rules matter

Key Takeaway

A stock exchange is a marketplace where investors buy and sell stocks under shared rules.

12. What Is the New York Stock Exchange?

Overview

The New York Stock Exchange (NYSE) is one of the major stock exchanges in the United States. Many large, well-known public companies list their shares on the NYSE. Being "listed on the NYSE" means the company's stock meets the exchange's listing requirements and trades there.

People see "NYSE" on stock quotes, finance websites, and market news. It is common to hear "the NYSE" when people talk about big, established companies and the overall stock market.

If you misunderstand the NYSE, you might think it is a government office or a company that "controls" stock prices. In reality, it is a marketplace that helps trading happen efficiently.

Example

Two companies are both public. One lists on the NYSE and the other lists on NASDAQ. Investors can still buy and sell both, but each one trades on its own exchange.

Why This Matters

- Many major U.S. companies trade on the NYSE
- "Listed on NYSE" is a common phrase in stock market conversations
- It helps you recognize where a company's stock trades

Key Takeaway

The NYSE is a major U.S. exchange where shares of many public companies are traded.

13. What Is NASDAQ?

Overview

NASDAQ (National Association of Securities Dealers Automated Quotations) is a fully electronic, dealer-based stock exchange in the United States. Unlike traditional floor-based exchanges, NASDAQ operates through a network of computers and market participants (market makers) that facilitate trading.

NASDAQ is best known for listing many technology and growth-oriented companies, but it also includes firms across healthcare, consumer goods, finance, and more.

From a market structure standpoint, NASDAQ is classified as a quote-driven market, where multiple market makers continuously provide bid (buy) and ask (sell) prices, ensuring liquidity and efficient price discovery.

Example

A student looks up a company online and sees "NASDAQ: ABCD." That label tells the student which exchange the stock trades on.

Why This Matters

- NASDAQ plays a key role in liquidity provision through market makers
- The "NASDAQ: ____" label helps you identify where a stock is listed
- It builds your comfort reading stock quotes and market news

Key Takeaway

NASDAQ is a technology-driven, electronic stock exchange where multiple market participants interact through an automated system to buy and sell shares, enabling fast execution, liquidity, and efficient price discovery.

14. What Is the Primary Market?

Overview

The primary market is where new shares are sold for the first time. This is the moment when a company raises money by selling stock directly to investors as part of a new offering. A common example is an IPO (initial public offering), when a company first sells shares to the public.

People usually hear "primary market" when they hear about an IPO or a company "issuing new shares." The key idea is who receives the money: in the primary market, the company receives the money because the shares are newly created and sold.

If you do not understand the primary market, you might assume companies make money every time investors trade a stock. Most everyday stock trades happen later in the secondary market, not the primary market.

Example

A company goes public and sells newly issued shares to investors. The company receives the money from that sale, and the shares begin their life as publicly owned stock.

Why This Matters

- The primary market is how companies raise money by selling new shares
- People often think companies profit from every trade (usually they do not)
- It helps you understand what an IPO really means

Key Takeaway

The primary market is where a company sells new shares for the first time to raise money.

15. What Is the Secondary Market?

Overview

The secondary market is where investors buy and sell shares with each other after the shares already exist. This is what most people mean in everyday life when they say, "I bought a stock" or "I sold a stock." The trades happen between investors, and the company usually does not receive money from these trades.

People encounter the secondary market through brokerage accounts and investing apps, where orders are placed and matched on exchanges. The stock price you see each day is shaped mostly by secondary market trading.

If you misunderstand the secondary market, you might think your trade sends money to the company. In most cases, it does not. Your money goes to another investor who is selling shares, and you receive the shares in return.

Example

A company went public last year. Today, you buy 3 shares from another investor through your brokerage app. The company is not selling you new shares today. You are trading in the secondary market.

Why This Matters

- Most stock trading happens in the secondary market
- It explains why prices move every day based on investor decisions
- It clears up the common confusion about where your money goes when you buy stock

Key Takeaway

The secondary market is where investors trade existing shares with each other.

16. What Is Listing?

Overview

Listing refers to the formal process by which a company's shares are admitted for trading on a regulated exchange such as the New York Stock Exchange or NASDAQ. Once listed, the company's stock becomes part of a centralized, regulated marketplace where trades occur under strict rules governing transparency, disclosure, and investor protection.

A listed company transitions from a private ownership structure to a publicly tradable security, typically through an Initial Public Offering (IPO) or, in some cases, a direct listing.

You commonly see listing information on stock quote pages (it will show the exchange name), in company announcements, and in news that says "the company listed its shares" or "is seeking a listing."

If you do not understand listing, you might think any company can be traded like a stock. In reality, a company must meet certain rules to be listed on an exchange, and that listing tells investors where the shares trade and what standards the company follows.

Example

A company becomes public and gets listed on an exchange. After listing, investors can look up its ticker on that exchange and trade shares through brokerage accounts during market hours.

Why This Matters

- Listing helps investors know where a stock trades
- It signals that the company meets exchange standards
- It reduces confusion about what is "publicly traded" versus not

Key Takeaway

Listing means a company's stock is approved to trade on a stock exchange.

17. What Are Listing Requirements?

Overview

Listing requirements are the rules a company must meet to have its stock listed on a stock exchange. Exchanges set standards because investors need trust, transparency, and basic quality controls. These requirements can involve financial size, number of shares available to the public, company governance, and ongoing reporting.

You usually hear about listing requirements when a company plans to go public, when a company switches exchanges, or when news mentions a company is "at risk of delisting."

If you misunderstand listing requirements, you might assume listing is automatic. It is not. Exchanges use requirements to make sure listed companies follow certain expectations and keep investors informed.

Example

A company wants to list its shares on a major exchange. The exchange reviews the company's financials and reporting practices. If the company meets the standards, it can list. If it does not, it may need to improve first or choose a different marketplace.

Why This Matters

- Requirements help protect investors from low-quality or unclear listings
- Companies must keep meeting rules, not just meet them once
- Understanding this explains why some companies get delisted

Key Takeaway

Listing requirements are the standards a company must meet to trade on a stock exchange.

18. What Is an Initial Public Offering (IPO)?

Overview

An Initial Public Offering (IPO) is when a company sells its stock to the public for the first time. It is a major step because it turns a company into a publicly traded company and creates new shares (or sells existing ones) so investors can buy them. The IPO happens in the primary market, where the company raises money from the initial sale.

You see IPOs in headlines like "Company X files for an IPO" or "Company X priced its IPO." After the IPO, the stock begins trading more broadly, and investors can buy and sell shares in the secondary market.

If you misunderstand IPOs, you might think buying on IPO day guarantees profits. It does not. Prices can rise or fall quickly based on demand and expectations.

Example

A growing company wants money to expand. It launches an IPO and sells shares to public investors. The company receives money from that first sale. After that, investors trade the stock with each other, and the price moves based on what buyers and sellers agree on.

Why This Matters

- IPOs explain how companies first enter the stock market
- People often expect "easy money" from IPOs, which can lead to risky choices
- It helps you understand primary vs. secondary markets

Key Takeaway

An IPO is the first time a company sells stock to the public and becomes publicly traded.

19. What Is a Direct Listing?

Overview

A direct listing is a way for a company to become publicly traded without the traditional IPO process. Instead of selling a large batch of new shares first, the company allows existing shares (owned by early investors, employees, or founders) to be traded publicly on an exchange.

You might hear about direct listings when companies want to list shares without the same type of IPO roadshow and pricing process. The stock begins trading, and the market sets the price through buying and selling.

If you misunderstand direct listings, you might think the company is "not really public." It is public once its shares are listed and can be traded, but the path it took to get there is different from a traditional IPO.

Example

A company decides it does not want a traditional IPO. It lists on an exchange through a direct listing, and existing shareholders can sell shares to public investors once trading opens.

Why This Matters

- It's another way companies can enter the public stock market
- The early trading price is shaped heavily by supply and demand
- Understanding it prevents confusion when you see "direct listing" in news

Key Takeaway

A direct listing lets a company's existing shares begin trading publicly without a traditional IPO.

20. What Is Delisting?

Overview

Delisting means a company's stock is removed from a stock exchange, so it no longer trades on that exchange. Delisting can happen for many reasons, such as failing to meet listing requirements, merging with another company, or choosing to go private.

You may see delisting mentioned in news headlines, company notices, or warnings that a company is "at risk of being delisted." When a stock is delisted, it can become harder to trade, and it may move to a different trading venue depending on the situation.

If you do not understand delisting, you might assume a delisted company disappears overnight. It usually does not disappear, but trading access, visibility, and investor confidence can change significantly.

Example

A company's stock price stays very low for a long time and it fails an exchange rule. The exchange delists the stock. Investors may still be able to trade it somewhere else, but it is no longer on the major exchange it used to trade on.

Why This Matters

- Delisting can reduce liquidity and make trading harder
- It often signals financial stress or major change
- Understanding it helps you interpret risk warnings and headlines

Key Takeaway

Delisting means a stock is removed from a stock exchange and no longer trades there.

21. What Is a Brokerage Account?

Overview

A brokerage account is an account you use to buy and sell investments, such as stocks and funds. It is different from a bank account. A bank account is mainly for holding money and making payments. A brokerage account is mainly for investing.

People commonly see brokerage accounts inside investing apps, retirement rollover conversations, and when someone says, "I bought a stock." Even if you do not invest yet, you may hear this term when friends talk about investing or when you see ads for investing platforms.

If you misunderstand a brokerage account, you might treat it like a checking account or expect it to work the same way. A brokerage account can go up or down in value because investments move in price, and it may also have fees, rules, and tax forms connected to it.

Example

You deposit $200 into a brokerage account and buy shares of a company. Over the next month, the stock price changes. Your account value changes too, even though you did not add or remove money.

Why This Matters

- A brokerage account is the basic tool used for investing in stocks
- Confusing it with a bank account can lead to surprises about risk and taxes
- Understanding it helps you make clearer investing decisions

Key Takeaway

A brokerage account is an account designed for buying and selling investments.

22. What Is a Broker?

Overview

A broker is a person or company that helps investors buy and sell investments. In simple terms, a broker connects you to the stock market. When you place a trade in an investing app, a broker is involved in making that trade happen.

You encounter brokers when you open an investing account, when you see a company described as a "brokerage firm," or when you get account statements and confirmations after a trade.

If you misunderstand the word broker, you might think the broker "chooses your stocks." Some brokers offer advice, but many only provide the service of placing trades and holding your investments in your account.

Example

You click "buy" on a stock in your investing app. The broker sends your order to the market and helps complete the trade so you receive the shares.

Why This Matters

- Brokers are the middle step between you and the stock market
- Confusing brokers with "financial advisors" can lead to wrong expectations
- Knowing the broker's role helps you understand fees and account services

Key Takeaway

A broker is a person or company that helps you buy and sell investments.

23. What Is an Online Brokerage?

Overview

An online brokerage is a brokerage firm that lets you manage your investing account through a website or app. Instead of calling someone on the phone, you can place trades, view your holdings, and check your account value online.

People commonly encounter online brokerages through investing apps, retirement rollover choices, and "open an account" links on finance websites. These platforms often make investing feel easy because everything is one click away.

If you misunderstand online brokerages, you might assume "easy to trade" means "easy to profit." Online access removes friction, but it does not remove risk. Prices can still move quickly, and mistakes can still be costly.

Example

A teen turns 18 and opens an online brokerage account. They deposit money, buy a few shares, and check the price every day on their phone.

Why This Matters

- Online brokerages are the most common way people invest today
- Easy access can lead to impulsive buying and selling
- Understanding the tool helps you focus on learning, not clicking

Key Takeaway

An online brokerage is a broker you use through a website or app to trade investments.

24. What Is a Full-Service Broker?

Overview

A full-service broker is a brokerage firm (or broker) that offers more support than just placing trades. Full-service brokers may provide investing guidance, research, planning help, and personal service. Because more help is included, the costs are often higher than basic trading platforms.

You may encounter full-service brokers when families talk about "my broker," when someone mentions having a dedicated advisor, or when investors want help building a long-term plan instead of making all decisions alone.

If you misunderstand full-service brokers, you might assume they guarantee better results. More service can be helpful, but outcomes still depend on market performance, costs, and the quality of decisions.

Example

An investor wants help planning for retirement. They work with a full-service broker who explains choices, suggests a mix of investments, and checks in regularly, while charging higher fees for that service.

Why This Matters

- Full-service brokers can provide support and guidance
- Higher costs can reduce returns over time
- Understanding the difference helps you choose the level of help you need

Key Takeaway

A full-service broker offers trading plus extra guidance and services, often for higher fees.

25. What Is a Discount Broker?

Overview

A discount broker is a brokerage firm that focuses on low-cost trading and basic account services. It usually does not provide the same level of personal guidance as a full-service broker. The main goal is to make buying and selling investments cheaper and simpler.

People most often encounter discount brokers through popular investing apps and websites. These platforms usually provide tools, charts, and basic information, but they expect you to make the final decisions yourself.

If you misunderstand discount brokers, you might assume "discount" means lower quality or unsafe. The term mainly refers to pricing and service level. What matters is understanding what help is included and what is not.

Example

An investor wants to buy and hold a few stocks and funds without paying high fees. They use a discount broker, place trades online, and manage everything on their own.

Why This Matters

- Discount brokers can lower costs for investors
- Less guidance means you need to learn and double-check decisions
- Understanding the trade-off helps you choose wisely

Key Takeaway

A discount broker offers low-cost trading with fewer personalized services.

26. What Is Market Access?

Overview

Market access means your ability to place buy and sell orders in the stock market through a brokerage account. Most people do not trade "directly" on an exchange. They use a broker or online brokerage that connects their order to the market.

You see market access in real life when you open an investing app, choose a stock, and see the option to buy or sell. You may also notice it when certain trades are not allowed in an account, when trading is limited outside market hours, or when an account is restricted.

If you misunderstand market access, you might assume clicking "buy" always means an immediate trade at the price you see. In reality, access depends on the broker's systems, market hours, order types, and whether there is a matching buyer or seller.

Example

A student opens a brokerage account and tries to buy a stock at night. The app accepts the order, but it does not execute until the market opens and the broker can send the order to be matched.

Why This Matters

- Market access explains how your trades reach the market
- Confusion can lead to surprises about timing and prices
- It helps you understand why orders sometimes wait or do not fill right away

Key Takeaway

Market access is how you reach the stock market through a broker to place trades.

27. What Are Clearing and Settlement?

Overview

Clearing and settlement are the behind-the-scenes steps that make a stock trade official after you click buy or sell. Clearing confirms the details, and settlement is when shares and money are actually exchanged.

You don't usually see this because apps feel instant, but it shows up as "pending trades" or "unsettled funds."

If you misunderstand clearing and settlement, you might think a trade is finished the moment you press the button. The trade may be agreed upon quickly, but the official transfer happens through this process.

Example

You sell shares on Monday and expect to withdraw the money right away. Your account shows the sale, but the cash is still "unsettled," so the brokerage limits what you can do with it until settlement is complete.

Why This Matters

- It explains why money and shares may not be available instantly
- Misunderstanding can cause mistakes like trying to use unsettled cash too soon
- Knowing this helps you avoid account restrictions and confusion

Key Takeaway

Clearing and settlement are the steps that finalize a trade by transferring shares and money.

28. What Is the Settlement Period?

Overview

The settlement period is the post-trade processing window between the trade date (T)—when an order is executed—and the settlement date (T+N)—when legal ownership of securities transfers and cash is exchanged.

In U.S. equity markets, the standard settlement cycle is currently T+1, meaning settlement occurs one business day after the trade date. This cycle is governed by clearing and settlement infrastructure overseen by entities like the U.S. Securities and Exchange Commission and processed through clearinghouses such as the Depository Trust & Clearing Corporation (DTCC).

Example

You sell a stock on Monday (T).

The proceeds appear in your account immediately
But they are unsettled until Tuesday (T+1)
If you use those funds to buy another stock and sell it before Tuesday, you may trigger a violation

Why This Matters

- It affects when cash becomes fully available after a sale
- It helps explain "unsettled funds" messages in brokerage accounts
- Understanding it reduces trading mistakes and account flags

Key Takeaway

The settlement period is the short time it takes for a trade to be fully completed.

29. What Is Custody of Securities?

Overview

Custody of securities means who holds and safeguards your investments (your stocks, funds, or other securities) on your behalf. In most everyday investing, your brokerage account holds the shares for you electronically, tracks your ownership, and records what you own.

You see custody in real life when you receive account statements, tax forms, and trade confirmations that show what you own. It is also why you do not receive "paper stock certificates" in most modern investing. Your ownership is recorded digitally.

If you misunderstand custody, you might think your shares are "inside the app." The app is just the display. The custody and recordkeeping system is what actually tracks your ownership and protects it.

Example

You buy 2 shares of a company. You do not receive a physical paper certificate. Your brokerage records your ownership, and your account shows the shares as part of your holdings.

Why This Matters

- Custody explains how your ownership is tracked and protected
- It reduces worry about "where the shares are"
- Understanding it helps you read statements and recognize legitimate account records

Key Takeaway

Custody of securities is how your brokerage holds and records your investments safely for you.

30. What Are Account Types?

Overview

Account types are different kinds of brokerage accounts designed for different goals and rules. Some accounts are meant for general investing, while others are designed for long-term goals like retirement or education. The account type can affect taxes, withdrawal rules, and what features are available.

You encounter account types when you open a brokerage account and must choose between options like an individual account, joint account, or retirement account. You may also see different account labels inside the same brokerage login.

If you choose the wrong account type, you can create problems later, such as unexpected taxes, penalties, or restrictions on withdrawals. Even when the investments are the same, the account type can change the results.

Example

Two people buy the same stock. One buys it in a regular brokerage account. The other buys it in a retirement account. The stock may perform the same, but the tax rules and withdrawal rules can be very different.

Why This Matters

- Account types can change taxes and access to money
- Misunderstanding can lead to surprises when withdrawing or selling
- Knowing the purpose of each account helps you match investing to your goals

Key Takeaway

Account types are different brokerage account setups that affect rules, taxes, and how you use your investments.

31. What Is a Buy Order?

Overview

A buy order is a formal instruction submitted to a broker or trading platform to purchase a specified quantity of a security (such as a stock) under defined conditions. Once submitted, the order is routed to a trading venue like the NASDAQ or New York Stock Exchange, where it interacts with other market participants through an electronic order book.

A buy order does not guarantee execution at a specific price unless conditions are tightly defined. Execution depends on market liquidity, order type, and timing.

People encounter buy orders in investing apps when they tap "Buy," when they review an order preview screen, or when they see an order status like "filled," "partially filled," or "pending." If you ignore how buy orders work, you can end up buying at a higher price than expected or placing an order that does not go through at all.

Example

You decide to buy 2 shares of a company. You place a buy order. If sellers are available at your chosen conditions, your order fills and you become a shareholder of those 2 shares.

Why This Matters

- You use buy orders anytime you purchase a stock
- Confusion can lead to surprise prices or unfilled trades
- Understanding buy orders helps you trade more intentionally

Key Takeaway

A buy order is a structured trading instruction that defines how you enter a position in the market. Understanding order types, pricing, and execution mechanics helps you avoid unexpected prices and trade with greater precision.

32. What Is a Sell Order?

Overview

A sell order is a formal instruction submitted through a broker to dispose of (sell) a specified quantity of securities you own under defined conditions. The order is routed to a trading venue such as the NASDAQ or New York Stock Exchange, where it interacts with incoming buy orders through an electronic order book.

Like a buy order, a sell order does not guarantee a specific execution price unless you explicitly control it (e.g., with a limit order). Execution depends on market liquidity, order type, and prevailing bid prices.

People see sell orders when they tap "Sell," when they choose how many shares to sell, and when they receive a trade confirmation. If you misunderstand sell orders, you may sell at a lower price than you expected, especially during fast market moves.

Example

You own 5 shares and want to cash out. You place a sell order. If buyers are available at your chosen conditions, your order fills and you receive the sale proceeds in your account.

Why This Matters

- Sell orders decide how you exit an investment
- Mistakes can cause unexpected selling prices
- Understanding sell orders helps you control risk and timing

Key Takeaway

A sell order is a structured instruction to exit a position, where execution depends on market conditions and order type. Understanding its mechanics helps you manage risk, avoid unfavorable prices, and maintain control over your trading outcomes.

33. What Is a Market Order?

Overview

A market order is an order to buy or sell immediately at the best available price in the market. The main goal is speed, not price control. Because prices can change quickly, the final execution price may differ slightly from what you saw when placing the order. These orders are routed to exchanges like the NASDAQ or New York Stock Exchange and are filled against the current bid-ask spread.

People encounter market orders when an app shows "Market" as the default option. They are simple to use, but in fast-moving or low-liquidity markets, they can result in slippage (a different price than expected).

Example

A stock is showing $30. You place a market buy order for 1 share. Your order fills immediately, but the final price could be $30.05 or $30.20 if the price moves while your order is being filled.

Why This Matters

- Market orders are fast, but price is not guaranteed
- They can lead to surprises during rapid price changes
- Understanding this helps you avoid "I didn't mean to pay that much" moments

Key Takeaway

A market order executes immediately at the best available price, but that price is not guaranteed and can vary slightly based on market conditions and available liquidity.

34. What Is a Limit Order?

Overview

A limit order is an order to buy or sell a security only at a specified price or better. It gives you price control, unlike a market order, but it does not guarantee execution. The order is placed into the exchange's electronic order book (such as on NASDAQ or New York Stock Exchange) and waits until matching orders are available at your price.

People see limit orders on the order screen when they enter a specific price. A common misunderstanding is assuming the trade will always go through. In reality, the order will only execute if the market reaches your limit price and sufficient shares are available.

Example

A stock is trading around $50. You place a limit buy order at $48:

If the price drops to $48 and sellers are available → your order can fill
If the price never reaches $48 → your order remains unfilled

Even if the price touches $48 briefly, your order may not fill if other orders ahead of you get executed first.

Why This Matters

- Limit orders help you control the price you pay or receive
- They may not execute, which can frustrate people who expect instant trades
- Understanding limits helps you trade with more discipline

Key Takeaway

A limit order gives you control over the price at which you trade, but execution depends on market conditions—so it may not fill if your price is never reached.

35. What Is a Stop Order?

Overview

A stop order is an order that becomes active only after a stock reaches a specific trigger price (stop price). It is commonly used as a risk management tool, especially to limit losses or protect gains. Once the stop price is reached, a standard stop order converts into a market order, meaning it executes quickly at the best available price—not a guaranteed price. These orders are processed through exchanges like the NASDAQ or New York Stock Exchange.

People encounter stop orders when they see options like "Stop," "Stop-Loss," or "Trigger price" in trading apps. A key misunderstanding is thinking the stop price is the execution price—it is only the activation point.

Example

You buy a stock at $40 and set a stop order at $36:

If the price drops to $36 → the stop is triggered
Your sell order becomes a market order
If the price is falling quickly, you might sell at $35.80 or lower—not exactly $36

Why This Matters

- Stop orders are common tools for managing downside risk
- People often confuse the trigger price with a guaranteed sell price
- Understanding stops helps you avoid surprises during market drops

Key Takeaway

A stop order activates when a stock hits a trigger price, and then it tries to trade.

36. What Is a Stop-Loss Order?

Overview

A stop-loss order is a type of stop order used to limit how much you can lose on a stock. You choose a stop price, and if the stock falls to that trigger price, the order activates and tries to sell. The goal is protection, not profit.

People commonly see stop-loss options in brokerage apps under "risk tools" or "exit strategies." It can be misunderstood as a guaranteed selling price. It is not. The stop price is the trigger. The final selling price can be a little lower (especially if the stock is dropping fast).

Example

You buy a stock at $50. You set a stop-loss at $45. If the stock drops to $45, the stop-loss triggers and your sell order activates. If the price is falling quickly, your sale might fill at $44.80 or $44.50 instead of exactly $45.

Why This Matters

- Stop-loss orders are a common way investors try to control losses
- Confusing the trigger price with a guaranteed price can create surprises
- Understanding stop-loss orders helps you manage risk more calmly

Key Takeaway

A stop-loss order triggers a sell when a stock hits a chosen price to help limit losses.

37. What Is Order Execution?

Overview

Order execution is the process of your buy or sell order actually being completed. When an order executes, it means a match was found and a trade happened. Your order can be executed instantly, partially, or not at all, depending on the market and the order type.

You see execution in real life when your app shows "filled," "partially filled," "pending," or "canceled," and when you receive a trade confirmation showing the final price and number of shares.

If you do not understand execution, you may assume clicking "buy" means you definitely bought at the price you saw. In fast markets, execution price and timing can differ from what you expected.

Example

You place an order to buy 10 shares. Only 6 shares are available at that moment at your conditions, so 6 execute now and 4 remain pending until more sellers appear (or the order expires).

Why This Matters

- Execution explains why your final price can differ from the screen price
- Misunderstanding can lead to confusion about "why my order didn't go through"
- It helps you interpret order status messages correctly

Key Takeaway

Order execution is when your order is actually completed as a real trade.

38. What Is Order Routing?

Overview

Order routing is how your broker sends your order to a place where it can be matched and executed. Your order might be routed to a stock exchange, a market-making firm, or another trading venue, depending on the broker's system and the type of order.

You typically notice routing only indirectly, such as in trade confirmations, account disclosures, or settings that mention "routing" or "best execution." Most investors do not choose the route manually, but routing affects how quickly and at what price an order may fill.

If you ignore routing, you might assume every order goes to the NYSE or NASDAQ. In reality, brokers can route orders in different ways while still aiming for a fair execution.

Example

Two people place the same market order for the same stock using different brokerages. One order routes to an exchange and fills immediately. The other routes differently and fills a second later at a slightly different price because the market moved.

Why This Matters

- Routing can affect speed and the final price you receive
- It helps explain why two people might get slightly different fills
- Understanding it makes broker disclosures and confirmations less confusing

Key Takeaway

Order routing is how your broker sends your trade to a venue where it can be executed.

39. What Are Bid and Ask?

Overview

Bid and ask are the two main prices you see for a stock at any moment. The bid is the highest price someone is currently willing to pay to buy the stock. The ask is the lowest price someone is currently willing to accept to sell the stock.

You see bid and ask on quote screens in brokerage apps, especially when you switch to "detailed quote" or when you place a limit order. Many beginners assume there is only one "true price." The truth is there are buyers and sellers with different prices, and trades happen when they agree.

Example

A stock quote shows: Bid $19.98 and Ask $20.02. If you place a market buy, you will usually buy near the ask because that is the price sellers are offering. If you place a market sell, you will usually sell near the bid because that is what buyers are offering.

Why This Matters

- Bid and ask explain how trades happen in real time
- Confusing them can lead to "why did I pay more than the price I saw?"
- Understanding them helps you place smarter limit orders

Key Takeaway

The bid is what buyers offer, and the ask is what sellers want.

40. What Is the Bid-Ask Spread?

Overview

The bid-ask spread is the difference between the bid price and the ask price. It is a small "gap" that exists because buyers and sellers do not always agree on the same price. A smaller spread usually means a stock is easier to trade quickly, while a bigger spread can mean trading may cost more or be less smooth.

You notice the spread when you look at a stock's quote and see two different prices, or when you place a trade and realize the buy price and sell price are not identical. Some people think the spread is a fee charged by the app. It is not exactly a fee, but it can feel like a cost because you often buy at the ask and sell at the bid.

Example

Bid $50.00 and Ask $50.10 means the spread is $0.10. If you buy and then immediately sell, you might lose around $0.10 per share just because of the spread, even if the market did not move.

Why This Matters

- The spread affects what it costs to get in and out of a stock quickly
- Big spreads can surprise beginners with worse-than-expected prices
- Knowing the spread helps you choose order types more carefully

Key Takeaway

The bid-ask spread is the gap between what buyers pay and what sellers accept.

41. What Is Market Price?

Overview

Market price is the current price a stock is trading at right now. It is the price buyers and sellers agree on when trades happen. This price can change every second because new orders are always coming in.

You see market price in brokerage apps, on finance websites, and in headlines like "the stock is up 3% today." Many people assume market price is the "true value" of a company. It is not. It is simply the current trading price based on what people are willing to pay and accept in that moment.

If you misunderstand market price, you might panic when it drops or get overly excited when it rises. The market price is a snapshot, not a guarantee of what the company is worth long term.

Example

A stock traded at $40 yesterday. Today, after news comes out, buyers are willing to pay $44 and sellers accept $44, so the market price becomes $44.

Why This Matters

- Market price is what you actually buy and sell at
- People confuse price with "real value," which can lead to emotional decisions
- Understanding market price helps you stay calm during daily moves

Key Takeaway

Market price is the current trading price that buyers and sellers agree on right now.

42. What Is Price Discovery?

Overview

Price discovery is the process of figuring out a stock's price through buying and selling. Each trade is like a mini vote: buyers show what they will pay, sellers show what they will accept, and the market price updates based on those decisions.

You encounter price discovery during big news days (earnings, major announcements), market openings, and fast-moving periods when prices jump or drop. People often think a stock price is "set" by one person or one company. It is not. Price discovery happens because thousands or millions of participants are making decisions at the same time.

If you ignore price discovery, price changes can feel random. But many moves are the market reacting to new information and changing expectations.

Example

A company reports strong profits. Many buyers rush in, willing to pay more. Sellers raise their asking price. Trades happen at higher prices, and the market "discovers" a new price level.

Why This Matters

- It explains why prices change when news or expectations change
- It reduces the feeling that markets are "rigged" or mysterious
- Understanding it helps you interpret price movement more logically

Key Takeaway

Price discovery is how the market finds a stock's price through real trades.

43. What Is Supply and Demand?

Overview

Supply and demand explains why stock prices move. Demand is how many people want to buy. Supply is how many people want to sell. When demand is stronger than supply, prices tend to rise. When supply is stronger than demand, prices tend to fall.

You see supply and demand in real life when a stock "jumps" after good news (more buyers than sellers) or "drops" after bad news (more sellers than buyers). People often assume prices move only because a company changed overnight. In reality, prices can move simply because more people want to buy or sell at that moment.

If you misunderstand supply and demand, you might blame every price drop on "the company failing," even when the move is driven by short-term trading behavior.

Example

A stock is at $30. Suddenly, many investors want to buy, but not many want to sell at $30. Buyers offer $31, then $32. The price rises because demand is higher than supply at the old price.

Why This Matters

- Supply and demand drives daily price movement
- Misunderstanding it can cause panic during normal price swings
- Knowing this helps you interpret "why the price moved" more clearly

Key Takeaway

Stock prices move because supply and demand change every moment.

44. What Is Liquidity?

Overview

Liquidity means how easy it is to buy or sell a stock quickly without causing a big price change. A stock with high liquidity has many buyers and sellers, so trades happen smoothly. A stock with low liquidity may be harder to trade, and prices can move more sharply when orders are placed.

Liquidity is often reflected in how fast your order fills and how small the gap is between the bid and ask price. Stocks with higher trading volume usually have better liquidity.

You notice liquidity when your trade fills instantly versus when it sits waiting, or when there are large price gaps. Not all stocks trade the same—some are much easier to trade than others.

If you ignore liquidity, you may end up paying more when buying or receiving less when selling, especially in thinly traded stocks.

Example

You try to sell a stock. In one stock, your sale fills immediately near the quoted price. In another stock, very few buyers exist, so you have to accept a lower price to sell quickly. That second stock has lower liquidity.

Why This Matters

- Liquidity affects how smoothly you can enter and exit a stock
- Low liquidity can create worse prices and more frustration
- Understanding liquidity helps you avoid surprises when trading

Key Takeaway

Liquidity is how easily you can buy or sell a stock without big price changes.

45. What Is Trading Volume?

Overview

Trading volume is the number of shares traded during a specific period, such as a day. It shows how active a stock is. Higher volume means more buyers and sellers are involved, while lower volume means less activity and interest.

Volume also gives a quick sense of how easy it is to trade a stock. Stocks with higher volume are usually easier to buy or sell, while lower-volume stocks may have fewer buyers and sellers at any moment.

You'll see volume on stock charts, quote pages, and market summaries. People sometimes assume high volume means a stock is "good." It does not—volume only shows activity, not quality.

If you misunderstand volume, you might chase a stock just because it is popular today. Volume is a clue about activity, not a guarantee of future performance.

Example

A stock usually trades 200,000 shares per day. After big news, it trades 3,000,000 shares in one day. That jump in volume shows many more people are buying and selling than usual.

Why This Matters

- Volume helps you understand how active a stock is
- Low volume can be linked to liquidity issues and wider spreads
- Understanding volume helps you read stock screens and charts more confidently

Key Takeaway

Trading volume is the number of shares traded in a given time period.

46. What Is Volatility?

Overview

Volatility means how much and how quickly a stock's price moves up and down. A highly volatile stock can swing sharply in a short time, while a low-volatility stock tends to move more steadily. Volatility is not "good" or "bad"—it simply describes how bumpy the price movement is.

Volatility is often seen in daily percentage changes and is commonly measured over time to understand how much prices typically fluctuate. Stocks with higher volatility tend to react more strongly to news, earnings, or market changes.

You notice volatility when a stock jumps 8% one day and drops 6% the next, or when people say "the market is volatile."

If you ignore volatility, you might invest money you need soon into something that can drop quickly, leading to stress or rushed decisions.

Example

A student buys a fast-growing stock. In one week, it rises from $20 to $24, then falls to $19 after bad news. The stock might still be a strong company, but the price movement is very volatile.

Why This Matters

- Volatility affects how risky a stock feels day to day
- People often confuse volatility with "the company is failing"
- Understanding it helps you choose investments that match your comfort level

Key Takeaway

Volatility is how much a stock's price swings up and down over time.

47. What Is Price Efficiency?

Overview

Price efficiency means how quickly and accurately a stock's price reflects available information. In an efficient market, when new information appears—good or bad—the price adjusts quickly because many buyers and sellers react fast.

You notice price efficiency on earnings days or big news days, when prices move almost immediately after an announcement. Many beginners think prices move "randomly." Often, prices are reacting to new information, new expectations, or surprises compared to what investors expected.

If you misunderstand price efficiency, you may assume you can easily "outsmart" the market with obvious news that everyone else already saw.

Example

A company reports profits much higher than expected. Within minutes, many investors buy, and the stock price jumps. That quick adjustment is an example of price efficiency at work.

Why This Matters

- Prices often change quickly after new information
- It helps explain why "easy wins" are harder than they look
- Understanding it encourages realistic expectations about picking stocks

Key Takeaway

Price efficiency means stock prices adjust quickly when new information becomes known.

48. What Is Market Depth?

Overview

Market depth describes how many buy and sell orders exist at different prices for a stock. A "deep" market has lots of orders waiting at many price levels, so big trades can happen with smaller price changes. A "shallow" market has fewer orders, so even a medium-sized trade can move the price more.

You usually do not see market depth unless you view a detailed order book, but you feel it when your order fills smoothly versus when your trade pushes the price up or down.

If you ignore market depth, you might be surprised when a trade executes in pieces at different prices or when a stock price jumps because there were not many orders available.

Example

Two stocks both trade around $10. One has many buyers and sellers lined up at $9.99, $10.00, $10.01, and more. The other has very few orders near $10. A large buy order barely moves the first stock, but pushes the second stock up quickly because there are not enough sellers nearby.

Why This Matters

- Market depth affects how smoothly trades happen
- Low depth can cause bigger price moves from normal orders
- Understanding it helps explain "why the price moved when I traded"

Key Takeaway

Market depth is how many buy and sell orders exist at different prices for a stock.

49. What Are Thinly Traded Stocks?

Overview

Thinly traded stocks are stocks that have low trading activity—meaning not many shares are bought and sold regularly. These stocks often have lower liquidity, wider bid-ask spreads, and larger price swings when orders hit the market.

You may notice a thinly traded stock when the quote shows a wide gap between bid and ask, when your order takes longer to fill, or when the price jumps sharply on small amounts of trading.

If you do not recognize thin trading, you might assume you can buy and sell easily like a popular stock, but then get stuck with an unfilled order or a worse price than expected.

Example

A stock trades only a small number of shares each day. You place a market order to buy, and the price jumps higher as your order fills because there were not many sellers available near the last price.

Why This Matters

- Thinly traded stocks can be harder and more expensive to trade
- They can have bigger, faster price swings
- Understanding this helps you avoid surprise execution prices

Key Takeaway

Thinly traded stocks have low trading activity, which can make prices jumpy and trades harder.

50. What Is Price Impact?

Overview

Price impact is the amount a stock's price moves because of a trade. In a highly liquid stock with strong market depth, a normal-sized trade may have little price impact. In a thinly traded stock, even a smaller trade can push the price up or down noticeably.

You feel price impact when you buy and the price rises as your order fills, or when you sell and the price falls while your shares are being sold. This is more likely when the stock has low liquidity or a wide bid-ask spread.

If you ignore price impact, you might blame "bad luck" or assume your broker did something wrong, when the real reason is that your trade itself moved the market.

Example

A person tries to buy a large number of shares in a low-volume stock. There are not many sellers near the current price, so the order consumes the available shares and keeps buying at higher prices. The final average price ends up higher than expected because the trade created its own price impact.

Why This Matters

- Price impact can change the price you actually get
- It is stronger in thinly traded, low-liquidity stocks
- Understanding it helps you trade with more realistic expectations

Key Takeaway

Price impact is how much a trade itself pushes a stock's price up or down.

51. What Is Market Capitalization?

Overview

Market capitalization (often called "market cap") is the total market value of a company's stock. It answers a simple question: How big is this company in the stock market?

Market Cap = Stock Price × Number of Shares Outstanding

You will see market cap on stock quote pages, investing apps, and lists that label companies as large-cap, mid-cap, or small-cap. Many people confuse market cap with a company's revenue or profit. It is not the same. Revenue is money the company earns from sales. Market cap is what investors, as a group, currently think the company is worth based on its stock price.

Market cap matters because it affects how people think about risk and stability. Larger companies often have more steady businesses and more trading activity, while smaller companies can grow faster but may have bigger price swings. If you ignore market cap, you might compare two companies using only stock price and accidentally assume a $10 stock is "smaller" than a $200 stock, even if the $10 stock company is actually bigger overall.

Why This Matters

- Market cap is a quick way to understand company size in the stock market
- Many people make mistakes by comparing only stock prices instead of total company value
- Knowing market cap helps you understand risk, stability, and why some stocks move more than others

Key Takeaway

Market capitalization is the total value of a company's stock, found by multiplying the stock price by the number of shares.

52. What Are Large-Cap Stocks?

Overview

Large-cap stocks are shares of very large companies with high market value. "Cap" is short for market capitalization (market value). Large-cap companies are often well-known, have established businesses, and are followed closely by investors and the news.

You'll see "large-cap" in stock screeners, mutual funds, index funds, and retirement plans (like "large-cap fund").

Large-cap stocks tend to be more stable and widely traded, but they can still go up or down. Understanding this helps you avoid judging companies just by share price and instead focus on overall size and risk.

Example

Two stocks look very different by price: one is $25 per share and another is $250 per share. The $25 stock could still be a large-cap company if it has many shares outstanding and a huge total market value. A student who understands large-cap focuses on the company's overall size, not just the share price.

Why This Matters

- "Large-cap" shows up often in funds, retirement plans, and investing tools
- People confuse share price with company size and make wrong comparisons
- Understanding large-cap helps you judge stability, risk, and expectations more realistically

Key Takeaway

Large-cap stocks are stocks of very large companies based on total market value.

53. What Are Mid-Cap Stocks?

Overview

Mid-cap stocks are stocks of companies with a medium-sized market capitalization—bigger than small companies, but smaller than the biggest large-cap companies. Mid-cap companies are often in a "growth stage," meaning they may still be expanding, entering new markets, or becoming more well-known.

People commonly see "mid-cap" in investing apps, stock screeners, and fund descriptions like "mid-cap fund" or "mid-cap growth." Mid-cap companies can sometimes grow faster than large-caps, but they can also have more ups and downs in price.

This matters because if you invest without noticing the size category, you might be surprised by how much the stock moves or by how sensitive it is to the economy or competition. Understanding mid-cap helps you set better expectations about risk and potential growth

Example

A company is well past the startup stage and has steady sales, but it is not yet one of the biggest names in the market. Investors call it a mid-cap. Over a few years, if it grows a lot, it may eventually become a large-cap company.

Why This Matters

- "Mid-cap" appears often in fund choices and investing categories
- People may expect mid-caps to act like large-caps and get surprised by bigger swings
- Understanding mid-cap helps you match investments to your risk comfort and goals

Key Takeaway

Mid-cap stocks are stocks of medium-sized companies based on total market value.

54. What Are Small-Cap Stocks?

Overview

Small-cap stocks are stocks of companies with a smaller market capitalization, meaning their total stock-market value is smaller than large-cap and mid-cap companies. These companies are often earlier in their growth journey. Some are building their brand, expanding into new regions, or trying to become a bigger player in their industry.

You will see "small-cap" in investing apps, stock screeners, and in fund names like "small-cap fund." Small-cap stocks can sometimes grow faster than bigger companies, but they can also be more volatile, meaning prices may jump up and down more.

If you ignore the "small-cap" label, you might be surprised by bigger price swings or assume the company is "small" just because the stock price is low. Stock price alone does not tell you company size—market cap does.

Example

A company has a stock price of $12, but it has many shares and a market cap that still makes it a small-cap. The stock moves 6% in one day after a small piece of news because fewer investors trade it compared to a giant company stock.

Why This Matters

- Small-cap categories show up often in funds and investing tools
- People confuse low stock price with "small company" and misjudge risk
- Understanding small-cap helps you set realistic expectations about volatility and growth

Key Takeaway

Small-cap stocks are stocks of smaller companies based on total market value.

55. What Are Micro-Cap Stocks?

Overview

Micro-cap stocks are stocks of very small public companies, usually smaller than typical small-cap companies. Because these companies are so small, their stocks can be less liquid (harder to trade quickly), have wider bid-ask spreads, and experience bigger price swings.

You might see micro-cap stocks when browsing "penny stock" conversations online, scanning lists of small public companies, or looking at stocks that trade with very low daily volume.

If you misunderstand micro-cap stocks, you might assume they are "cheap and easy money" because the share price can look low. The bigger issue is not the price—it is that trading can be difficult and risky when fewer buyers and sellers are involved.

Example

A micro-cap stock shows a price of $2.50. You try to buy, but the bid and ask prices are far apart, and your order fills at a worse price than expected because there are not many sellers.

Why This Matters

- Micro-cap stocks can be harder to buy and sell at predictable prices
- Low trading activity can create big price jumps on small news
- Understanding micro-cap helps you avoid confusing "low price" with "low risk"

Key Takeaway

Micro-cap stocks are stocks of very small public companies and can be harder to trade smoothly.

56. What Are Outstanding Shares?

Overview

Outstanding shares are the total number of shares a company currently has in existence and owned by shareholders. This number matters because it is part of how market capitalization is calculated:

Market Cap = Stock Price × Outstanding Shares.

You will see outstanding shares on stock information pages, company filings, and finance apps that show company stats. Beginners often confuse outstanding shares with "shares I personally own." Outstanding shares means all shares owned by everyone combined, not your personal amount.

If you ignore outstanding shares, you might make a wrong comparison between two companies by looking only at the stock price. A $20 stock can represent a massive company if it has billions of shares, while a $200 stock can represent a smaller company if it has fewer shares.

Why This Matters

- Outstanding shares help determine market cap and company size
- People often misjudge company size by looking only at share price
- Understanding this makes stock comparisons more accurate and less confusing

Key Takeaway

Outstanding shares are the total number of shares a company has issued and that investors currently own.

57. What Is Public Float?

Overview

Public float (often just called "float") is the number of a company's shares that are available for the public to buy and sell in the stock market. It usually does not include shares that are tightly held by insiders (like founders and executives) or other long-term holders who are not likely to trade often.

You will see float on stock information pages and in market discussions like "this stock has a small float" or "float is increasing." Float matters because it affects how easily a stock can trade and how much the price can swing when many people try to buy or sell at the same time. If the float is small, the price may move faster because fewer shares are available in the market.

If you ignore float, you might be surprised by sudden price jumps or drops, especially in smaller companies where fewer shares are actively traded.

Example

A company has 100 million shares outstanding, but only 60 million are available for public trading. That 60 million is the public float. If a lot of new buyers show up at once, the stock price may rise quickly because there are fewer shares available to satisfy demand.

Why This Matters

- Float affects how easily a stock trades and how jumpy the price can be
- A small float can make price moves feel extreme during busy trading days
- Understanding float helps explain big price swings that seem "out of nowhere"

Key Takeaway

Public float is the number of shares available for public trading.

58. What Is Free Float?

Overview

Free float is very similar to public float. It usually refers to the shares that are freely available to trade, excluding shares held by insiders, governments, or other owners who are unlikely to sell often. In many everyday stock screens, "free float" and "public float" are used in nearly the same way.

You may encounter "free float" when looking at index rules, stock data pages, or fund descriptions that mention "free-float adjusted" weighting. The idea is simple: the market pays attention to the shares that can actually move around in normal trading.

If you do not understand free float, you might assume all outstanding shares trade equally. They do not. Some shares are basically "locked up" or rarely traded.

Example

A company has many shares outstanding, but a large portion is held by founders and is not likely to trade. The free float is the remaining shares that everyday investors can buy and sell more easily.

Why This Matters

- Free float helps explain how much of a company's stock is really tradable
- Low free float can increase volatility and widen bid-ask spreads
- It helps you understand why some stocks move sharply on normal-sized trades

Key Takeaway

Free float is the portion of shares that are realistically available for everyday trading.

59. What Are Share Classes?

Overview

Share classes are different "types" of shares a company issues. Even though each share represents ownership, different classes can come with different rights. The most common difference is voting power, but classes can also differ in rules or special features.

You may see share classes when a stock quote shows letters after the company name, such as "Class A" or "Class B." Many people assume all shares of one company are identical. With share classes, that is not always true.

If you do not pay attention to share classes, you might buy shares thinking you have the same voting rights as another class of shareholders, when you do not.

Example

A company has Class A shares that give 1 vote per share and Class B shares that give 10 votes per share. Two investors can own the same dollar amount of stock, but one may have much more voting power because they own the higher-vote class.

Why This Matters

- Share classes can change who controls the company's decisions
- Investors may misunderstand what rights they get when they buy a stock
- Understanding share classes helps you read stock listings more accurately

Key Takeaway

Share classes are different types of shares that can come with different rights, especially voting rights.

60. What Are Dual-Class Shares?

Overview

Dual-class shares mean a company has two main classes of stock with different voting rights. Often, one class is sold to the public with lower voting power, while another class is held by founders or insiders with higher voting power. This structure can let founders keep control of company decisions even if they do not own most of the total shares.

You may hear "dual-class" in business news, in discussions about company control. Some people think owning stock automatically means having strong influence. With dual-class shares, public investors may have limited voting power compared to insiders.

If you ignore dual-class shares, you might misunderstand who really controls the company and how much say public shareholders have.

Example

A founder owns special shares with 10 votes per share, while public shares have 1 vote per share. Even if the founder owns less than half of all shares, the founder can still control most votes and guide major decisions.

Why This Matters

- Dual-class shares can keep control in the hands of founders/ insiders
- Investors may assume ownership always equals influence, which is not always true
- Understanding this helps you know what "shareholder voting" really means

Key Takeaway

Dual-class shares are two classes of stock where insiders often keep more voting power than public shareholders.

61. What Is Investment Return?

Overview

Investment return is the money you make (or lose) from an investment over time. It includes any increase in the investment's price and any cash you receive, such as dividends. If your investment grows in value, you have a positive return. If it drops, you have a negative return.

You commonly see return in investing apps as "total return," "gain/loss," or "performance." People also talk about returns when comparing investing choices, like "Which investment gives better returns?"

If you misunderstand return, you might focus only on the stock price and ignore dividends, or you might assume a return is guaranteed. Returns can change, and short-term returns can be very different from long-term returns.

Example

You invest $100 in a stock. A year later, your shares are worth $110 and you received $2 in dividends. Your total return is $12 on a $100 investment.

Why This Matters

- Returns help you measure how your investment performed
- People often forget dividends when thinking about returns
- Understanding return helps you compare investments more accurately

Key Takeaway

Investment return is the money you gain or lose from an investment over time.

62. What Are Capital Gains?

Overview

Capital gains are the profit you make when you sell an investment for more than you paid for it. If you sell for less than your purchase price, the difference is a capital loss.

A gain becomes real only when you sell (called a realized gain). Until then, it is an unrealized or "paper" gain. Gains may also be taxed depending on how long you held the investment.

You'll see capital gains in brokerage accounts, tax forms, and investing summaries. Many people confuse price increases with actual profit, but the gain is not locked in until you sell.

If you misunderstand capital gains, you might think you've made money just because prices are up, even though you haven't sold.

Example

You buy a share for $30. Two months later, you sell it for $42. Your capital gain is $12.

Why This Matters

- Capital gains are a main way stock investors make money
- People confuse "paper gains" with real gains they can spend
- Understanding capital gains helps you understand why selling decisions matter

Key Takeaway

A capital gain is the profit you make when you sell an investment for more than you paid for it. It is calculated as the selling price minus your purchase price. The gain becomes real only when you sell the investment; until then, it is an unrealized (paper) gain.

63. What Are Dividends?

Overview

Dividends are cash payments some companies distribute to shareholders. They are one way investors can earn income from a stock without selling it. Not all companies pay dividends—some reinvest profits back into the business for growth.

Dividends are usually paid on a regular schedule (such as quarterly) and are often quoted as a per-share amount or as a dividend yield (a percentage of the stock price).

You'll see dividends in brokerage accounts as "dividend payment," "cash distribution," or "income." Investors often look for "dividend stocks" when they want steady income.

If you misunderstand dividends, you might think they are "free money." Dividends come from company profits, and the stock price can still move up or down.

Example

You own 10 shares of a company. The company pays a $0.50 dividend per share. You receive $5.00 in your brokerage account.

Why This Matters

- Dividends are a common source of stock income
- People assume every stock pays dividends, which is not true
- Understanding dividends helps you read account activity and total returns

Key Takeaway

Dividends are cash payments that some companies distribute to shareholders as a share of their profits. They are typically paid on a per-share basis and may be issued regularly, such as quarterly, depending on the company's policy.

64. What Is Dividend Yield?

Overview

Dividend yield is a percentage that shows how much dividend income a stock pays compared to its current stock price. It is a quick way to compare dividend-paying stocks by income level. Dividend yield changes when either the dividend changes or the stock price changes.

You commonly see dividend yield on stock quote pages and in fund descriptions. Beginners often think a higher yield always means a better deal. A very high yield can sometimes happen because the stock price fell sharply, which may signal higher risk.

If you misunderstand dividend yield, you might chase high yields without noticing the company's stability or whether the dividend is likely to continue.

Example

A stock costs $50 per share and pays $2 per share each year in dividends.

Dividend yield = $2 ÷ $50 = 0.04 = 4%.

Why This Matters

- Yield helps you estimate dividend income relative to price
- People chase high yields without checking risk and sustainability
- Understanding yield helps you compare dividend stocks more clearly

Key Takeaway

Dividend yield shows dividend income as a percentage of the stock's current price.

65. What Is Dividend Policy?

Overview

Dividend policy is a company's approach to paying dividends—how much it pays, how often it pays, and whether it plans to increase, reduce, or stop dividends over time. Some companies aim to pay steady dividends. Others pay little or none and focus on growth.

You see dividend policy when companies announce dividend changes, when investors discuss "dividend growth," or when a company explains how it uses profits (pay dividends, invest in growth, buy back stock, or reduce debt).

If you misunderstand dividend policy, you might assume dividends will always stay the same. Companies can change dividend payments, especially if profits fall or business priorities shift.

Example

A company pays a quarterly dividend and has a policy of trying to raise the dividend a little each year. After a tough year, the company pauses increases to keep more cash for the business.

Why This Matters

- Dividend policy affects how reliable dividend income may be
- People assume dividends are permanent, but they can change
- Understanding policy helps you interpret dividend announcements and investor expectations

Key Takeaway

Dividend policy is a company's plan for if, when, and how it pays dividends to shareholders.

66. What Is Total Return?

Overview

Total return is the full amount of money you gain or lose from an investment over time. It combines price change (capital gains or losses) and cash income you receive (like dividends). In other words, total return answers: How much did I really make (or lose) overall?

People commonly see total return in brokerage apps and retirement accounts as "total return," "performance," or "gain/loss including dividends." Many beginners look only at the stock price and forget dividends. That can make an investment look worse or better than it truly is. Total return is the more complete picture.

If you ignore total return, you might compare two investments incorrectly. One stock might have a smaller price increase but paid dividends, and it could outperform a stock with a bigger price increase but no dividends.

Example

You buy a stock for $100. One year later, the stock is worth $108, and you received $3 in dividends.

Your total return is $11 ($8 price gain + $3 dividends).

Why This Matters

- Total return is what investors actually care about: the full result
- People often forget dividends and misjudge performance
- Understanding total return helps you compare investments more accurately

Key Takeaway

Total return is your overall gain or loss from an investment, including both price changes and dividends.

67. What Is Reinvestment?

Overview

Reinvestment means using money you earn from an investment to buy more of that investment instead of spending the money. In the stock market, reinvestment often happens when dividends are used to buy more shares. Over time, reinvesting can help your investment grow faster because your gains start earning gains too.

People commonly see reinvestment in brokerage accounts through settings like "reinvest dividends," in retirement accounts where earnings stay invested, and in account statements that show dividends being used to purchase additional shares automatically.

If you ignore reinvestment, you may miss out on growth that comes from building more shares over time. Some people also get confused when they see extra shares appear and think the broker "added" something randomly. It is often reinvestment at work.

Example

You own 20 shares of a stock. The company pays a dividend, and you receive $10. Instead of taking the $10 in cash, you reinvest it and buy a small fraction of an extra share. Next time a dividend is paid, you earn dividends on slightly more shares than before.

Why This Matters

- Reinvestment is a common way long-term investors grow their holdings
- People may forget that dividends can be used to buy more shares
- Understanding reinvestment helps explain how compounding happens in investing

Key Takeaway

Reinvestment means using investment earnings to buy more shares instead of taking the cash.

68. What Is a Holding Period?

Overview

A holding period is how long you keep an investment before you sell it. It can be a day, a month, or many years. The holding period matters because it changes how you experience price movement and, in many cases, how taxes may apply to gains.

You will hear "holding period" when people talk about short-term vs long-term investing, when discussing investing strategy, and when reading brokerage summaries that show when you bought and sold.

If you misunderstand the holding period, you might judge an investment too quickly or panic during normal short-term drops. Many investments look "bad" in the short run but can look very different over years.

Example

Two investors buy the same stock. One sells after two weeks because the price dips. The other holds for five years and benefits from the company's growth over time. Their results differ mainly because their holding periods were different.

Why This Matters

- Holding period shapes how risky an investment feels
- Short holding periods can lead to emotional, reactive decisions
- Understanding it helps you match investing to your goals and timeline

Key Takeaway

A holding period is the length of time you own an investment before selling it.

69. What Is Compounding?

Overview

Compounding is when your money grows, and then the growth itself starts growing too. In investing, compounding happens when returns (like price gains or dividends) stay invested, so future returns are earned on a larger amount than before.

People encounter compounding when they hear phrases like "let your money compound," when they reinvest dividends, or when they look at long-term investment charts that curve upward over time. Compounding is one of the biggest reasons long-term investing can work, even with small amounts.

If you misunderstand compounding, you may expect fast results and quit too early. Compounding often looks slow at first, then becomes more powerful later.

Example

You invest $500. After a year, it grows to $550. If you keep it invested, the next year you are earning returns on $550, not $500. Over many years, that growing base can make a big difference.

Why This Matters

- Compounding is a key reason time matters in investing
- People underestimate how much small amounts can grow over many years
- Understanding compounding encourages patience and consistency

Key Takeaway

Compounding is growth on top of growth when returns stay invested.

70. What Are Long-Term Returns?

Overview

Long-term returns are the results you earn from an investment over a long period, such as several years or decades. Long-term returns include both price changes and dividends, and they smooth out many short-term ups and downs.

You see long-term returns discussed in retirement planning, index fund discussions, and advice like "don't judge the market by one week." Investors focus on long-term returns because the stock market can be very noisy in the short run but more meaningful over longer time frames.

If you ignore long-term returns, you may make decisions based on short-term fear or excitement—buying high when everyone is excited and selling low when everyone is scared.

Example

A stock drops 10% in a month. A short-term view makes it feel like a disaster. Over ten years, that same stock might still deliver strong long-term returns if the company grows and the investor stays invested.

Why This Matters

- Long-term returns are what matter most for goals like retirement
- Short-term market moves can lead to emotional mistakes
- Understanding long-term returns supports patience and better habits

Key Takeaway

Long-term returns are the overall results of an investment measured over many years.

71. What Is a Bull Market?

Overview

A bull market is a period when the stock market is generally rising over time. During a bull market, many stocks trend upward, and investors often feel more confident about the future. A bull market is not just one good day or one good week. It usually describes a longer stretch where prices are climbing overall.

You'll hear the term in news, investing apps, and conversations about strong market performance. Bull markets often come with optimism, but they still include temporary drops and pullbacks along the way.

If you misunderstand a bull market, you might assume prices will only go up and take on too much risk. Bull markets can include pullbacks and sudden drops along the way.

Example

Over the past year, the overall market trend has been upward. Your investment account shows steady growth, and many companies' stock prices are higher than they were months ago. News articles describe this period as a bull market because the general direction has been rising.

Why This Matters

- The term comes up often when people talk about market "good times" and long upward trends
- If you assume bull markets last forever, you might invest too aggressively or panic when a normal drop happens
- Understanding bull markets helps you keep expectations realistic and stay disciplined

Key Takeaway

A bull market is a long period when stock prices are generally rising.

72. What Is a Bear Market?

Overview

A bear market is a period when the stock market is generally falling over time. It is the opposite of a bull market. During a bear market, many stocks drop, and investors often feel more nervous or cautious. A bear market is not just one bad day. It usually describes a longer stretch where prices trend downward overall.

People commonly hear "bear market" in news headlines, when retirement accounts show declines, or when friends say, "The market is down this year." Bear markets can happen for many reasons, such as worries about the economy, company profits, or global events.

If you misunderstand a bear market, you might assume the market is "broken" forever and sell out in panic. Bear markets are painful, but they are also a normal part of how markets move over time.

Example

A student invests money and sees their account drop month after month. News reports keep saying major indexes are down for the year. People start avoiding investing because they feel scared. That longer down period is a bear market.

Why This Matters

- Bear markets show up in headlines and affect retirement and investing accounts
- Panic selling is a common mistake when people do not understand bear markets
- Understanding bear markets helps you stay calmer during down periods

Key Takeaway

A bear market is a long period when stock prices are generally falling.

73. What Is a Market Cycle?

Overview

A market cycle is the repeating pattern of ups and downs in the stock market over time. Markets do not move in a straight line. They usually go through phases, such as growth periods (bull markets), pullbacks, slower periods, and sometimes longer declines (bear markets).

People notice market cycles when they hear "the market always goes through cycles" or when they look at long-term charts that show rising trends with dips along the way. You may also notice it when your account feels great one year and disappointing the next.

If you do not understand market cycles, you might think every drop means you made a bad decision. In reality, short-term declines can be part of a normal cycle. Understanding the cycle helps you keep perspective.

Example

Over several years, the market rises strongly, then drops for a few months, then rises again. A long-term investor expects these shifts and does not panic during the down parts because they understand markets move in cycles.

Why This Matters

- Market cycles explain why "good years" and "bad years" both happen
- People make emotional mistakes when they expect the market to only go up
- Understanding cycles supports patience and better long-term habits

Key Takeaway

A market cycle is the normal pattern of market rises and declines over time.

74. What Is a Market Correction?

Overview

A market correction is a noticeable drop in prices after the market has been rising, often described as the market "cooling off." A correction is usually smaller than a bear market and can happen even when the long-term trend is still upward.

People encounter the word "correction" in headlines like "the market entered correction territory," in app alerts about market declines, or when investors say, "This drop is normal." Corrections can happen because prices rose too fast, investors take profits, or new worries show up.

If you misunderstand corrections, you might treat a normal drop like a full crash and sell in fear. Corrections can feel scary, but they are common in the stock market.

Example

The market rises steadily for months. Then, over a few weeks, it drops and many stocks fall from recent highs. News calls it a correction. After some time, the market stabilizes and may start rising again.

Why This Matters

- Corrections happen often and show up in market news
- People panic-sell when they do not realize corrections are common
- Understanding corrections helps you avoid overreacting to normal declines

Key Takeaway

A market correction is a temporary drop in prices that often happens after a period of rising markets.

75. What Is a Market Crash?

Overview

A market crash is a sudden, sharp drop in stock prices over a short period of time. Crashes are more extreme than normal daily declines and often happen when fear spreads quickly and many investors rush to sell at once.

People hear "crash" in dramatic news coverage, in phrases like "stocks plunged," or when charts show a steep drop. Crashes can be triggered by major surprises, financial stress, or large-scale uncertainty.

If you misunderstand crashes, you might assume the market will never recover, or you might make rushed decisions at the worst time. Crashes are rare compared to normal ups and downs, but they can feel intense because they happen fast.

Example

A major piece of unexpected bad news hits the market. Within days, prices drop sharply and headlines use words like "plunge" and "panic." Many investors sell quickly, pushing prices down even more. That rapid, steep drop is a market crash.

Why This Matters

- Crashes create strong emotions and can lead to impulsive decisions
- People often confuse crashes with normal corrections
- Understanding what a crash is helps you interpret headlines more calmly

Key Takeaway

A market crash is a sudden, steep fall in stock prices over a short time.

76. What Is Market Recovery?

Overview

Market recovery is the period after a major market drop when stock prices begin to rise again and move back toward earlier levels. A recovery can happen quickly or slowly, and it is usually not a straight line upward. There can be ups and downs along the way.

People notice market recovery in headlines like "markets rebound," in charts that show the market climbing after a fall, and in retirement accounts that start improving after a tough stretch. Many people think recovery means everything goes back to normal immediately. In reality, recoveries can take time and can include setbacks.

If you misunderstand recovery, you may sell during a downturn and miss the early part of the rebound. Market recoveries are one reason long-term investors try not to make decisions based only on short-term fear.

Example

The market drops sharply for several months. Then it stabilizes, and over the next year it gradually rises again. Your account balance starts increasing after being down. That climbing period is the market recovery.

Why This Matters

- "Recovery" shows up often after corrections, bear markets, and crashes
- People who panic-sell may miss the rebound
- Understanding recovery supports patience and long-term thinking

Key Takeaway

Market recovery is the period when the market rises again after a significant drop.

77. What Are Economic Cycles?

Overview

Economic cycles are the normal ups and downs in the economy over time. The economy can go through periods of stronger growth, slower growth, and sometimes recession. These shifts can affect jobs, business profits, consumer spending, and investor confidence.

People encounter economic cycles in news about "the economy is slowing," "growth is strong," "recession fears," or "unemployment is rising." Even if you do not follow business news, you can feel economic cycles through changes in hiring, wages, prices, and how confident people feel about spending.

If you ignore economic cycles, stock market moves can feel confusing. Company profits and investor expectations often change as the economy changes, which can push stock prices up or down.

Example

During a strong economy, people buy more products and businesses earn higher profits. Stocks may rise because investors expect growth. Later, if the economy slows and people spend less, company profits can drop and stock prices can fall.

Why This Matters

- Economic cycles influence company performance and investor mood
- People confuse market drops with "bad investing" when it may be part of a cycle
- Understanding cycles helps you keep perspective during ups and downs

Key Takeaway

Economic cycles are the normal periods of growth and slowdown that affect businesses and markets.

78. What Is Interest Rate Impact?

Overview

Interest rate impact means that changes in interest rates can affect stock prices and the overall stock market. Interest rates influence borrowing costs for companies and consumers. When rates rise, loans and credit become more expensive. When rates fall, borrowing is cheaper.

You encounter this term in headlines like "markets reacted to rate hikes" or "stocks rose as rates fell." You may also feel it personally through mortgage rates, car loans, credit card interest, and student loan rates.

If you do not understand interest rate impact, market moves can feel random. Investors often change what they are willing to pay for stocks when borrowing costs and economic expectations change.

Example

Interest rates rise. A company that borrows money to expand now faces higher interest costs, which can reduce profits. Investors may value the stock less, so the stock price drops even if the company's products did not change overnight.

Why This Matters

- Interest rate news often moves markets quickly
- Rising rates can squeeze company profits and consumer spending
- Understanding this helps you interpret why stocks react to "rate" headlines

Key Takeaway

Interest rate changes can push stock prices up or down by affecting borrowing costs and expectations.

79. What Is Inflation Impact?

Overview

Inflation impact means inflation can affect stock prices and investing results. Inflation is when prices for goods and services rise over time, so money buys less than before. Inflation can raise costs for companies (materials, wages, shipping) and also change what consumers can afford.

People encounter inflation in everyday life at the grocery store, gas station, rent increases, and price changes on bills. In the market, you see it in headlines like "stocks fell on inflation worries" or "inflation cooled."

If you ignore inflation impact, you might focus only on "my investment went up" and forget that inflation can reduce what those gains can actually buy. Inflation is one reason investors care about long-term growth, not just saving in cash.

Example

Inflation rises and everyday costs increase. A company's costs go up too, so profits may shrink unless it can raise prices. Investors may lower what they are willing to pay for the stock, and the price can drop.

Why This Matters

- Inflation affects both your daily budget and company profits
- Ignoring inflation can make "returns" feel bigger than they are in real buying power
- Understanding inflation helps you see why markets react to inflation news

Key Takeaway

Inflation can influence stock prices by changing costs, profits, and what your returns can buy.

80. What Is Global Market Influence?

Overview

Global market influence means events in other countries can affect the U.S. stock market and individual stocks. Many companies operate globally—selling products, sourcing materials, and relying on international supply chains—so global news can impact their performance.

You'll see this in headlines about oil prices, geopolitical events, currency changes, or economic slowdowns abroad. Even if you invest only in U.S. stocks, global developments still matter.

If you ignore global influence, market moves can seem confusing. A stock may rise or fall not because of company news, but due to changes in global conditions affecting costs, demand, or investor sentiment.

Example

A company sells a large portion of its products overseas. If that region's economy slows, sales may drop. Investors may expect lower profits and sell the stock, pushing the price down—even though nothing changed in the company's U.S. business.

Why This Matters

- The stock market reacts to worldwide events, not just local news
- Many companies depend on global customers and global costs
- Understanding this helps you make sense of market moves that seem unrelated

Key Takeaway

Global events can affect stock prices because companies and investors are connected worldwide.

81. What Are Earnings?

Overview

Earnings are a company's profit over a period of time after it pays its expenses. In simple terms, earnings answer: Did the company make money, and how much? Earnings are not the same as revenue. Revenue is the total money a company brings in from sales. Earnings are what is left after costs are paid.

You will hear about earnings when companies report results each quarter, when the news says "the company beat earnings expectations," or when stock prices jump after an "earnings report." Investors pay close attention because earnings help them judge how healthy the business is and how it might perform in the future.

Example

A company sold $1,000,000 worth of products this quarter (revenue). After paying employees, rent, materials, and other costs, it has $120,000 left. That $120,000 is earnings (profit) for the quarter. If investors expected $200,000, the stock might fall because earnings were lower than expected, even though revenue was strong.

Why This Matters

- Earnings reports are major events that can move stock prices quickly
- People often confuse revenue with profit and misjudge company strength
- Understanding earnings helps you interpret news and avoid emotional reactions to price moves

Key Takeaway

Earnings are a company's profit after expenses, and they are a key signal of business performance.

82. What Are Earnings Reports?

Overview

Earnings reports are the regular updates public companies share to tell investors how the business performed over a period of time, often every three months (a quarter). These reports usually include key numbers like revenue, profit (or loss), and other important business details.

You encounter earnings reports in market news ("earnings season"), in apps that show an "E" date on a stock chart, and when a stock price jumps or drops right after results are released. Many people think prices move because earnings are "good" or "bad" in general. Often, prices move based on whether results were better or worse than what investors expected.

If you ignore earnings reports, stock price moves can feel random and stressful, especially when a stock suddenly changes direction after a report.

Example

A company reports earnings today. It made a profit, but it was less than investors expected. Even though the company "made money," the stock drops because the market wanted stronger results.

Why This Matters

- Earnings reports are major events that can move stock prices quickly
- People confuse "profit" with "meeting expectations" and get surprised by price reactions
- Understanding earnings reports helps you interpret market headlines and avoid panic

Key Takeaway

Earnings reports are regular company updates that show financial performance and often move stock prices.

83. What Is Revenue?

Overview

Revenue is the total money a company brings in from selling its products or services. It is often called "sales." Revenue does not mean profit. It is the top-line number before subtracting costs like wages, rent, materials, and marketing.

You see revenue in earnings reports, business news, and phrases like "revenue grew 12%." People often assume higher revenue automatically means a company is doing great. But a company can have high revenue and still lose money if expenses are even higher.

If you misunderstand revenue, you might think a company is successful just because sales are big, without checking whether the company keeps any money after paying its bills.

Example

A company sells $5 million worth of products this quarter. That $5 million is revenue. If it spent $5.2 million to run the business, it would still have a loss even with high revenue.

Why This Matters

- Revenue shows how much business is coming in, but not whether the company is profitable
- Confusing revenue with profit can lead to wrong conclusions about company health
- Understanding revenue helps you read financial news more accurately

Key Takeaway

Revenue is the total money a company earns from sales before expenses.

84. What Is Profit?

Overview

Profit is the money a company has left after paying all its costs and expenses. It is what remains after subtracting items like salaries, rent, materials, interest, and taxes from revenue. When people say a company "made money," they usually mean it earned a profit.

Profit can be shown in different ways, such as gross profit (after basic production costs) and net profit (after all expenses). Investors often focus on net profit because it reflects what the company actually keeps.

You see profit in earnings reports, news headlines like "profits fell," and discussions about how efficiently a company turns sales into earnings. A company can have strong sales but still have low profit or even losses if expenses are high.

If you misunderstand profit, you might overlook warning signs like rising costs or shrinking margins.

Example

A company has $1,000,000 in revenue. After paying $900,000 in total expenses, it has $100,000 left. That $100,000 is profit.

Why This Matters

- Profit is a key sign of business health
- Confusing popularity or revenue with profit can lead to bad investing assumptions
- Understanding profit helps you judge whether a company is actually earning money

Key Takeaway

Profit is what's left after a company pays all expenses from its revenue.

85. What Are Financial Statements?

Overview

Financial statements are the main documents companies use to show their financial performance and condition. For public companies, these statements are shared regularly so investors can evaluate the business. The most common financial statements are:

- Income statement (shows revenue and profit over a period)
- Balance sheet (shows what the company owns and owes at a point in time)
- Cash flow statement (shows how cash moved in and out of the business)

You encounter financial statements through earnings reports, investing websites, business class materials, and news summaries that mention "cash flow," "debt," or "margins." Many people only focus on stock price and ignore these statements, but financial statements explain what is happening inside the company.

If you misunderstand financial statements, you might rely only on hype or headlines and miss whether a company is actually growing safely, taking on too much debt, or burning cash.

Why This Matters

- Financial statements are the foundation of company information for investors
- People who ignore them can be misled by headlines or short-term price movement
- Understanding them helps you make smarter, calmer investing decisions

Key Takeaway

Financial statements are the key reports that show how a company earns money, what it owns and owes, and how cash moves.

86. What Is Valuation?

Overview

Valuation is an estimate of what a company is worth. In the stock market, it helps answer whether a stock looks "cheap" or "expensive" based on the company's performance and future potential—not just its share price.

You'll see valuation discussed in news, apps, and comparisons between companies. A common mistake is thinking a low-priced stock is cheap. A $10 stock can be expensive if the business is weak, while a $200 stock can be reasonable if the company is strong and growing.

If you ignore valuation, you might buy based on hype or price alone and be surprised when the stock falls because expectations were too high.

Example

Two companies each have a $50 stock price. One company earns strong profits every year. The other company loses money. Even with the same stock price, their valuations can be very different because investors judge their business strength and future potential differently.

Why This Matters

- Valuation shows up in almost every investing discussion about whether a stock is "worth it"
- People confuse stock price with "cheap," which leads to bad comparisons
- Understanding valuation helps you think beyond hype and focus on the business

Key Takeaway

Valuation is how investors estimate what a company is worth, not just what one share costs.

87. What Is the Price-to-Earnings (P/E) Ratio?

Overview

The price-to-earnings (P/E) ratio is a common valuation number that compares a company's stock price to its earnings. It helps investors quickly compare how expensive a stock looks relative to how much profit the company is making. A higher P/E often means investors expect more future growth. A lower P/E can mean the stock is cheaper, or it can signal worries about the company.

You will see P/E ratio on stock quote pages, in screeners, and in headlines like "the stock trades at a high P/E." A common mistake is thinking a high P/E is automatically bad or a low P/E is automatically good. Context matters: growth, industry, and earnings stability can all affect what a "normal" P/E looks like.

If you ignore P/E, you may miss that two stocks with similar prices can be valued very differently because one company earns far more profit than the other. For example, Company A's stock price is $60 and it earns $3 per share. P/E = 60 ÷ 3 = 20. Company B's stock price is also $60 but it earns $1 per share. P/E = 60 ÷ 1 = 60. Both stocks cost $60, but Company B is priced much higher compared to its earnings.

Why This Matters

- P/E shows up constantly in investing apps and market commentary
- People misuse P/E by treating it like a simple "buy/sell" signal
- Understanding P/E helps you compare stocks more intelligently

Key Takeaway

The P/E ratio compares a stock's price to its earnings to give a quick view of valuation.

88. What Are Growth Stocks?

Overview

Growth stocks are shares of companies expected to grow faster than average. These companies focus on expanding sales, gaining customers, and reinvesting profits back into the business, so they often pay little or no dividends.

You'll hear about growth stocks in fund names, market news, and discussions about high-growth companies. While they can rise quickly when expectations are strong, they can also fall sharply if growth slows or sentiment changes.

If you don't recognize growth stocks, you may be surprised by their higher volatility and strong reactions to earnings updates.

Example

A company is expanding quickly and investors believe its future profits will be much higher. Many investors buy the stock based on that future potential. If the company reports slower growth than expected, the stock may drop quickly because expectations were high.

Why This Matters

- Growth stocks are popular and often discussed in investing media
- They can be more volatile because expectations are a big part of the price
- Understanding growth stocks helps you set realistic expectations about ups and downs

Key Takeaway

Growth stocks are stocks of companies expected to grow faster than average, often with bigger price swings.

89. What Are Value Stocks?

Overview

Value stocks are stocks that investors believe are priced lower than the company's real strength or long-term potential. Value investors look for companies that seem "undervalued" compared to their earnings, assets, or stability. Value stocks often come from mature companies, and some pay dividends, but not always.

You will see "value" in fund names ("value fund"), in stock screeners, and in discussions like "value stocks are back." A common misunderstanding is thinking value stocks are always safe. A stock can look cheap for a reason, such as weak growth or business problems.

If you misunderstand value stocks, you might buy something just because it seems "cheap," without understanding why the market is cautious.

Example

A company has steady profits, but its stock price has fallen because investors are worried about the economy. Some investors see it as a value stock and buy because they believe the market is being too negative and the company will recover over time.

Why This Matters

- Value vs growth is a common way people describe investing styles
- People confuse "cheap" with "good," which can lead to mistakes
- Understanding value stocks helps you think about price compared to business strength

Key Takeaway

Value stocks are stocks that investors believe are priced lower than the company's true long-term value.

90. What Are Market Expectations?

Overview

Market expectations are what investors, as a group, believe will happen in the future for a company or the overall market. Stock prices do not move only based on what happened today. They often move based on whether reality matches, beats, or disappoints expectations.

You see market expectations in earnings season ("beat expectations"), in phrases like "priced in," and in stock reactions that seem confusing ("the company had good news but the stock fell"). That can happen when the good news was already expected, or when investors wanted even better results.

If you ignore expectations, you may feel confused by price moves and assume markets make no sense. Understanding expectations helps you interpret why prices react the way they do.

Example

Investors expect a company to earn $2.00 per share this quarter. The company reports $2.05, which is slightly better, and the stock rises. But if investors secretly hoped for $2.30, the stock might fall even though earnings increased—because expectations were not met.

Why This Matters

- Expectations drive many short-term price moves
- People get confused when "good news" leads to a falling stock
- Understanding expectations helps you read headlines and price reactions more calmly

Key Takeaway

Market expectations are the market's shared beliefs about the future, and prices often move when reality differs from those expectations.

91. What Is Market Risk?

Overview

Market risk is the risk that the overall stock market declines, causing many stocks to fall at the same time. Even strong companies can drop in price when investors are worried or selling broadly. This is different from company risk, which affects just one business.

You'll notice market risk when headlines mention broad declines or when your portfolio falls even without bad news from your investments. It also explains why diversified portfolios can still go down during market-wide downturns.

If you misunderstand market risk, you might blame a single stock or decision for losses that are actually affecting the entire market, which can lead to poor investment decisions.

Example

You own shares of several different companies in different industries. One week, news about the economy causes many investors to sell stocks broadly. Most stocks fall together, and your portfolio drops even though none of your companies released major negative announcements. That drop is market risk in action.

Why This Matters

- Market risk affects many stocks at once, even good companies
- People often confuse market-wide drops with a problem in one specific stock
- Understanding market risk helps you stay calmer and avoid emotional decisions during downturns

Key Takeaway

Market risk is the chance that the whole market drops and pulls many stocks down together.

92. What Is Company-Specific Risk?

Overview

Company-specific risk is the risk that one particular company faces problems that hurt its stock price. These issues can include poor management decisions, falling sales, product failures, lawsuits, or strong competition. Unlike market risk, this affects one company even if the overall market is doing well.

You'll notice this when a single stock drops after bad earnings, a leadership change, or negative news, while other stocks remain stable.

If you ignore company-specific risk, you might invest too heavily in one stock and face large losses from a single event.

Example

A company reports lower profits than expected and also warns that sales may slow next quarter. Even though the overall market is up that day, this company's stock falls because the problem is specific to that business.

Why This Matters

- It explains why one stock can drop even when the market is rising
- People who invest heavily in one company can take big hits from one event
- Understanding it helps you think about spreading risk across multiple stocks

Key Takeaway

Company-specific risk is the chance that a problem inside one company hurts its stock price.

93. What Is Systemic Risk?

Overview

Systemic risk is the risk that a problem in the financial system or economy harms many companies and markets at the same time. It is bigger than one company or one industry. Systemic risk can spread quickly because banks, businesses, investors, and markets are connected.

People encounter systemic risk in headlines about financial crises, major recessions, widespread banking stress, or events that cause broad panic selling. During systemic events, even strong companies can see their stock prices fall because investors are worried about the entire system.

If you misunderstand systemic risk, you may assume diversification will always protect you from market-wide drops. Diversification helps a lot with company-specific risk, but systemic risk can still pull many investments down together.

Example

A major financial crisis causes businesses to cut spending and banks to tighten lending. Investors sell stocks broadly, and many stocks fall at the same time, even across different industries.

Why This Matters

- Systemic risk explains broad market drops where "everything falls together"
- It helps you understand why even diversified portfolios can decline in major downturns
- Understanding it improves expectations about what investing risk really looks like

Key Takeaway

Systemic risk is the chance that a system-wide problem pulls many markets and stocks down together.

94. What Is Diversification?

Overview

Diversification means spreading your money across different investments so you are not depending on one company, one industry, or one outcome. The idea is simple: if one investment does poorly, others may hold up better, which can reduce the damage to your overall results.

People encounter diversification when they hear "don't put all your eggs in one basket," when they invest through funds that hold many stocks, or when they compare a portfolio with one stock versus a portfolio with many holdings.

If you ignore diversification, one company problem can hit your entire investment account. Diversification does not remove all risk, but it can reduce company-specific risk and help make results less extreme.

Example

Two investors each invest $1,000. One buys only one stock. The other spreads the $1,000 across several companies in different industries. When one company has bad news, the first investor's account drops a lot. The second investor's account drops less because only part of the money was in that one company.

Why This Matters

- Diversification is a core idea in investing and shows up in most advice
- People who concentrate in one stock take bigger company-specific risk
- Understanding it helps you build a more stable investing experience over time

Key Takeaway

Diversification means spreading investments so one company's problems do not ruin your results.

95. What Is Regulation?

Overview

Regulation means the rules and oversight that help keep the stock market fair, transparent, and trustworthy. In the U.S., regulation includes requirements for public companies to share information, rules against fraud and market manipulation, and standards for brokers and exchanges. Regulation does not guarantee you will make money. It is meant to reduce cheating and improve trust in how markets work.

You'll see regulation in action through company filings, trading halts, scam warnings, and regular earnings reports.

If you misunderstand regulation, you might assume the market is completely unprotected or, on the other side, assume regulation makes investing risk-free. The truth is in the middle: rules can reduce unfair behavior, but prices can still rise and fall.

Example

A public company must release regular financial reports so investors have consistent information. If the company lies or hides major facts, regulators can investigate and punish the company. That oversight helps investors trust the market more than they could without rules.

Why This Matters

- Regulation supports trust by requiring transparency and discouraging fraud
- People may fall for scams if they do not understand why rules and disclosures exist
- Understanding regulation helps you interpret filings, broker notices, and market rules

Key Takeaway

Regulation is the set of rules and oversight that helps keep stock markets fair and transparent.

96. What Is Market Oversight?

Overview

Market oversight is the monitoring and supervision that helps keep stock markets fair and orderly. It ensures that exchanges, brokers, and public companies follow rules and that trading remains transparent. It also looks for suspicious activity like fraud, insider trading, or manipulation.

In the U.S., oversight involves organizations like the Securities and Exchange Commission and the Financial Industry Regulatory Authority, which set rules and enforce them.

You encounter market oversight when you see trading halts, company filings, investigations in the news, or updates from your brokerage about rule changes.

If oversight is weak or misunderstood, trust in markets can fall, and investors may be more exposed to scams. Oversight does not remove risk, but it helps reduce unfair practices.

Example

A stock suddenly swings wildly on unusual activity. Trading is paused briefly, and regulators review what happened to check for manipulation or false information.

Why This Matters

- Oversight helps markets run smoothly and builds trust
- Without it, fraud and manipulation can spread more easily
- Understanding oversight helps you interpret halts, filings, and enforcement news

Key Takeaway

Market oversight is supervision that helps keep trading fair and orderly.

97. What Is Investor Protection?

Overview

Investor protection refers to the rules and safeguards that help investors receive honest information and fair treatment. This includes disclosure requirements, anti-fraud rules, and standards that brokers and companies must follow.

In the U.S., investor protection also includes coverage from the Securities Investor Protection Corporation (SIPC). SIPC helps protect customer accounts if a brokerage firm fails by covering missing cash and securities, up to certain limits. It does not protect against losses from market movements.

You encounter investor protection through brokerage disclosures, risk statements, company financial reports, and warnings about scams.

If investor protection is ignored, investors may be misled by false claims or hidden risks. While it cannot guarantee profits, it helps create a fairer and more transparent environment.

Example

If a brokerage firm goes out of business and customer assets are missing, SIPC works to return those assets or reimburse investors within its coverage limits.

Why This Matters

- Protection supports trust by requiring transparency
- It reduces the chances of investors being tricked by fraud
- Reduces the risk of fraud and misleading information

Key Takeaway

Investor protection is the system of rules and safeguards that helps investors receive fair treatment, honest information, and basic account protection.

98. What Is Behavioral Bias?

Overview

Behavioral bias is a common thinking pattern that can lead people to make poor investing decisions. It comes from human emotions and mental shortcuts—like fear, excitement, overconfidence, or following the crowd.

Common examples include fear of missing out (FOMO), loss aversion (feeling losses more strongly than gains), and overconfidence in one's decisions. These biases can influence when people buy, sell, or hold investments.

You see behavioral bias when people rush to buy a "hot" stock, panic during market drops, or hold onto losing investments hoping they recover.

If ignored, behavioral bias can lead to buying high, selling low, overtrading, or taking risks that don't match your goals.

Example

A stock jumps quickly and social media is hyping it. A new investor buys out of fear of missing out. A week later the stock falls, and the investor sells in panic, locking in a loss.

Why This Matters

- Bias shows up in real investing decisions every day
- It causes common mistakes like chasing hot stocks or panic selling
- Recognizing bias helps you act with more discipline

Key Takeaway

Behavioral bias is a mental shortcut or emotion that can push you into investing decisions you later regret.

99. What Is Market Efficiency?

Overview

Market efficiency means stock prices tend to reflect available information quickly. When new information becomes public, many buyers and sellers react, and the price adjusts.

There are different levels of efficiency—some investors believe prices reflect all public information, while others think certain insights or strategies can still add value. But in general, widely known information is usually already built into the price.

You see market efficiency on earnings days, major news events, or when prices move quickly before most people can react. This is why "easy profits" from obvious news are rare.

If misunderstood, investors may think they can consistently beat the market using simple headlines that everyone already knows.

Example

A company reports results after the market closes. Within minutes, the stock price jumps because investors quickly react and update what they are willing to pay.

Why This Matters

- It explains why prices can move fast on news
- It helps set realistic expectations about stock picking
- Understanding efficiency reduces frustration when "the market already moved"

Key Takeaway

Market efficiency means prices adjust quickly when new information becomes widely known, making it harder to gain an advantage from publicly available news.

100. What Is Stock Market Reality?

Overview

Stock market reality is the practical truth about how markets feel and behave in real life: prices move up and down, news can change opinions fast, and short-term results can be unpredictable. Long-term investing often rewards patience, but there are no guarantees.

People experience stock market reality when a "good company" stock still drops, when markets react to expectations instead of headlines, and when emotions make investing harder than math.

If stock market reality is ignored, investors may expect quick profits, get discouraged by normal declines, or make emotional moves that hurt results. Knowing the reality helps you invest with clearer expectations and less stress.

Example

An investor buys a strong company. The next month, the market drops due to economic worries and the stock falls too. The company did not suddenly become worthless—the market mood changed. The investor who understands reality stays calm and sticks to their plan.

Why This Matters

- Markets do not move in a straight line
- Short-term noise can lead to emotional decisions
- Understanding reality helps you stay disciplined and patient

Key Takeaway

Stock market reality is that prices swing, surprises happen, and patience matters more than perfect timing.

www.ingramcontent.com/pod-product-compliance
Lightning Source LLC
LaVergne TN
LVHW022112200926
848481LV00003B/1148

* 9 7 9 8 9 9 2 8 8 0 7 8 6 *